PASTOR
IS
MISSING

PRAY FOR PASTOR BERG

Alan M. Oberdeck

Inquiries and Book Orders should be addressed to:

Great Writers Media
Email: info@greatwritersmedia.com
Phone: (302) 918-5570

ISBN: 978-1-960939-98-2 (sc)
ISBN: 978-1-960939-99-9 (ebk)

CONTENTS

DEDICATION

THIS BOOK IS DEDICATED TO ALL OF the members of Christian Church congregations Worldwide who strive to be faithful to the Word of God as found in The Holy Bible. And to the Pastors who are called by God to faithfully serve these congregations to the best of their ability.

PREFACE

I WAS BORN AND BAPTIZED IN FEBRUARY of 1940. Some of my earliest memories were from the balcony of St. John's Lutheran Church in Edgerton, Wisconsin. In my early years, my faith was a very personal thing between God and myself, and I rarely mentioned it to anyone. The first time I prayed with anyone outside of a church setting was when my Pastor came and prayed at my bedside when I was in the hospital with polio.

After recovering from polio, I decided I would become a Lutheran Minister. Obviously, God had other plans for me. He gave me much success in another vocation. He also blessed me with the ability to serve Him in the congregations where I worshiped. The Lord in his time also blessed me with a wonderful wife and family.

During our married life together, we have been involved with three Mission Church start-ups and were active in two other mission congregations. We have also been active in other congregations. During our church life, I have been active as a church officer. Many times, this was as church president or head elder. This has led to several close relationships with church pastors providing a number of occasions to be involved in the inner workings of church. It is from this perspective that I write this book.

"*Pastor is Missing*" is a fiction based on many experiences from Pastors who I have known shared with me. I used a loving congregation as the setting to show the love and respect they have for their pastor. This loving congregation is made up of forgiven people, but were not always open to what the pastor feels he is called to do and where the factions within are not always supportive. Having a missing pastor allowed the president the necessity to search for a reason and the Pastor's diary gave him the opportunity to do just that. I named the Pastor Charles Daniel Berg as *Berg* translated in German means '*mountain*' and I wanted him to have a strong name.

When I write a story, I like to have readers who will read the story, give me feedback. Therefore, I would like to thank:

Virginia Daley
Rev. Ray Borchelt
Rev. Dr. David Bernthal
Rev. Dr. John W. Oberdeck

Sincerely,
Alan M. Oberdeck

WHAT HAPPENED TO PASTOR?

I DIDN'T KNOW WHAT TO EXPECT. I was standing there in front of the locked wooden door. At about eye level and to the right of the door was the shabby metal sign, the kind painted black with stamped raised white letters on it, identifying this door as the "*CHURCH OFFICE*". On the door itself was a brown plastic sign with letters carved into it indicating that inside I should find Rev. Charles '*Chuck*' Daniel Berg.

I knocked on the door again and was startled by the deep booming sound that broke the silence. The sound was generated by the hollowness of the cheap wooden door. I had the key to the lock in my hand but I really didn't want to have to use it. Letting myself into Pastor Chuck's locked office door seemed to me to be trespassing even though I had been asked to go in.

I waited, and when the booming stopped as before, only silence followed. I stood and waited, feeling like some messenger out of Milton's Epic Poem '*Paradise Lost*'. The part that came to mind was, "*He also serves who only stands and waits*". As I stood there, I thought about why I was there and what it was I was supposed to be doing.

It all started this afternoon.

Monday night had been the quarterly voters meeting for the second quarter of the year. I, having been elected president again, presided over the meeting and thought on the whole it went pretty well. There was the usual amount of bickering and grandstanding from a few of the *Old Guard*. There was the discussion following Pastors Report as to where the congregation was heading and the question "*Were we a dying church?*" Pastor took a number of hits from the *Old Guard*, but generally everyone was civil.

About 3:00 p.m. today, Helen, the pastor's wife, called me. I took the call at my Insurance Office. I normally don't accept personal calls at the business, but my secretary suggested it was urgent and that I should take it. Helen told me that the pastor didn't come home last night after the Voters Assembly Meeting. He had called her and said he would be staying late at the church and that she should not worry. *That was last night.* When he wasn't home this morning, she still wasn't too worried as he has a couch in the office and occasionally, when he has a hard sermon to prepare, will spend the night. When he didn't come home for lunch, that was when she began to worry. Helen had spent the afternoon trying to phone him at church with no success.

Pastor is over fifty and although in seemingly perfect health, she began to worry that maybe the pressures of late had caught up with him and he might be ill. To quote her, "*Heart attacks have happened to his father and uncles.*" She confided that she has been concerned about his health for some time now. She didn't want him to know just how concerned she was, so she asked if I would go, on some pretext, to the church and see if he was still there.

The way she put it was, "*just drop in on him, nothing special, just make sure he was all right, then call her to calm her fear.*" She sounded quite upset which was not like her. I promised I would drop what I was doing and go right over to the church. And I came right over, it took about forty-five minutes to get to the church from my Mid-Town Insurance Office. Usually, it takes about ten minutes, but the summer roadwork on the streets that I needed to take had just begun and the backups caused by the closing of lanes, many and slow to clear, slowed my travel time greatly.

I drove into the church driveway and up the little hill to where it curved beside the church. I was planning to turn the car around in the parking lot, park it by the side door of the church. Then I would then go inside and call Helen to tell her everything at church was okay. I would call her and reassure her Pastor was not there and ask her if he had come home yet. *That was the plan.*

My mind was so occupied with my supposed plan that it wasn't until I had turned my car around in the parking lot that I saw Pastor's car still parked where it had been the night before. I knew it hadn't been moved because last night, the lot was pretty full. He was late and had to park it in an unusual spot with the nose of the car buried under the boughs of a low spruce tree. I changed the direction of my car and drove to where Pastor's car was parked to check it out.

I left my car running with the transmission shifted into park as I got out of my car to take a look. Pastor's car was a blue 1996 Volkswagen Passat. The doors were still locked and nothing looked unnatural. I wondered if he had not moved his car because maybe his battery was low, after all, the car was only two years old, but the little red light indicating the alarm was set was brightly blinking. I concluded there was probably nothing wrong with the car. I drove to the parking area by the back door of the church and after parking, I entered and looked around a little. I found nothing.

There I stood still waiting to place my key in the lock and enter Pastor's Office. I had thought this would be so simple, but now I was afraid to open the door, afraid of what I might find! After all, he was over fifty and had been under a lot of pressure lately. I inserted the key in the lock, turned the knob, and began to open the door.

I pushed the door open slowly before me. Pastor's Office was laid out so as when you entered you looked straight at a five-foot-tall copy of a painting of the Lord holding a lantern and knocking at a door. The original is well known, but at that moment I couldn't for the life of me tell you the name of the painter or what the painting was called. On either side of the painting were doors, on one side to a small storage area, and the other side to a closet for Pastor's robes. The wall to the right as you enter is covered with shelves containing books and magazines for congregational reading.

Against the wall, immediately to the right, is the high-backed high-armed couch covered with an imitation leather material Pastor jokingly referred to as "*Pleather*". As I entered the office, I saw Pastor's desk and it was necessary to turn to the left to see the pastor's desk chair located behind the desk. The large desk itself is all wood veneer with massive ornamental carved legs. The edge of the top of the desk is carved with a rope design. The desk was stained with the color of walnut.

It is very regal looking and was a donation from the Ernst family. It had been used for years by Papa Ernst as his business desk at his hardware store. The chair behind the desk was of a modern design, comfortable and recently acquired from an office furniture store. In front of the desk, two padded armchairs were positioned. Behind the desk and chair was a medium sized window underneath which was a built-in credenza stained to match the desk and flanked on the sides with floor to ceiling bookshelves containing Pastor's reference library.

As I entered the office, I turned to my left out of habit. As I suspected it would be, the chair behind Pastor's desk was empty. I apprehensively turned to look at the couch and felt a wave of relief go through me as I found it was empty too. There was no answer to my knocking at the door because the office was empty! The car was there but the office was *empty*!

I walked over to the desk looking for Pastor's Daytime Planner to see if he had a meeting planned with a member of the congregation. I saw nothing like a Daytime Planner anywhere on the desk. I saw an open book with handwriting on one of the pages in the center of his desk, but his open bible was overlaying it so I kind of ignored it. I sat down in his chair, reached for the phone, and called Helen to report in.

The phone rang several times and finally was answered.

"Hello, Pastor Berg's residence."

"Hello, Helen?" I asked.

It didn't sound like Helen on the phone, and I wanted to verify to whom I was speaking.

"Yes, this is Helen Berg, can I help you with something?" she answered.

That was an unusual response considering she usually would recognize my voice and answer "*Why hello George*". She didn't recognize me! Could it be that the stress of coming here and not finding Pastor Chuck has affected me and my voice to the point of her not recognizing me?

"Helen, it is me! It is me, George Harrelson; I am at church in Pastor Chuck's office!"

"George, I didn't recognize your voice. Forgive me; I'm so upset I didn't recognize your voice! I have been trying to remain calm and handle things as if nothing has happened, but Chuck has never been gone this long without me knowing where he is!" she anxiously responded.

I had to answer her somehow, but how? I was at a loss for words. How can I tell her that he is not here, his car is here, but I have no idea where he is? I didn't want to alarm her further. Still, I had to ask her questions and from them she would figure out that he was not here.

"Helen, I am at church, and he is not here. I am looking for his Daytime Planner to see what appointments he might have this afternoon. Do you know where he keeps it?" I asked.

"It's not at church; he brought it home yesterday when he came home for supper. He is trying to go over our vacation plans and enter them into the Daytime Planner before he takes it back to church. I looked at it earlier and the today was open, however, this evening he has a counseling session at 8:00 with a young couple he will be marrying in a couple of months," she replied.

"Pastor Chuck isn't here anyplace; the church building was locked when I got here. He must have left with someone. His car is still parked where he parked it before last night's Voters Assembly Meeting," I answered as calmly as I could.

I was becoming more and more worried that some foul play had taken place.

"What do you want me to do?"

Helen was quiet for a moment and then through the phone came an answer, "Could you stay there for a while to wait until he returns? He wouldn't skip a counseling session with an engaged couple for anything. He should be there for the counseling session at 8:00. If he doesn't get back for that then something is wrong. When he gets back, please, don't let him know I brought you into this. I don't want him to know how worried I am. Could you just wait around until he comes back?" she asked in a pleading voice.

"I'll hang around the church and wait up here in his office for him," I answered.

That was probably the best action I could take for the time being. I was concerned but didn't want to have cried wolf either.

As I sat there in his office, I decided to check out the building one more time just to make sure there was no foul play, and he wasn't hidden away somewhere in a closet. I left the office and did a slow walk around the inside of the church building looking for signs of a struggle or some other indication of foul play. I looked in all the closets and even checked the attic.

I then did a complete circuit of the educational wing. I went outside and did a complete circuit of the facility looking behind the shrubs and any place someone could have hidden a body. I walked the trail through the large, wooded area. Again, I came up with nothing, no pastor, no sign of foul play, *just nothing*!

THE UNEXPECTED PHONE CALL

IT WAS A LITTLE PAST 7:00 WHEN I finished looking around. On my way back to pastor's office, I went into the sanctuary and sat down on the front pew to pray about the situation as I found it. Pastor was missing for now but would certainly show for the counseling session with the couple he was going to unite in Holy Matrimony. All I had to do was stay around until he returned so I could call Helen and tell her all was well.

I came back to Pastor Chuck's Office and sat down in his chair. There, before me a little to the center of his desk, on top of some papers, were sitting some books. There was an open book, the kind that you would write in to keep a record, a *Journal*. On top of that was an open Bible. Somehow, I was drawn to those open books.

I really hated to move anything on his desk, but the open Bible was on top of the open record book, and it drew me to it out of pure curiosity. Was this next Sunday's sermon in the making? Was it open to a special devotion for the morning? Of course, it could be only a random opening as he laid it down. I just knew I shouldn't peek, but I was tempted to lean over and peek a little bit.

The Bible was opened to the Gospel of St. Luke and the number 4 designating the beginning of the 4th chapter was circled. Verses 1 and 2 were underlined in red ink. I could not read them well as they were too far away. I decided if I were very careful, I could pick up the Bible and read what was underlined and the verses before and after. I decided if I were very careful, Pastor Chuck would never know I peeked.

I picked up the Bible and read: "4 Then Jesus, being filled with the Holy Spirit, returned from the Jordan and was led by the Spirit into the wilderness, 2 being tempted for forty days by the devil. And in those days, He ate nothing, and afterward, when they had ended, He was hungry." (Luke 4:1-2, NKJV) I set the Bible carefully aside.

As things would have it, though, when I picked up the Bible, the pages of the book it was lying on moved and I lost the spot where the book had been opened to. After I laid the open Bible to the side, I made sure not to lose the place it had been opened to. I paid special attention as to where the other book was so I could place it back after I picked it up. I picked it up and began to inspect it.

What I held in my hand was a rather thick bound book, approximately 8 by 10 inches in size on the face and close to an inch thick, a typical *Journal Book*. Between the covers the blue lined white pages at the back were devoid of printed words except for the page numbers printed in green ink on the upper edge of each page. I turned the book over and looked at the front cover. As I looked at the cover, I read the printed word *JOURNAL* embossed with green ink into the gray cloth-covered cardboard making up the covers. The pages in the front of the book were written full of Pastor Chuck's careful almost script-like handwriting.

I paged through the book until I came to the last page where there was writing. Here, I found Monday's date and the beginning of a description of the Voter's Assembly Meeting. He had begun one sentence, but for some reason he never completed the thought. This must have been the place the book was open to when he laid the open Bible on it. This must be Pastor Chuck's diary!

Have you ever picked up someone's diary and knew you shouldn't read it, but your curiosity got the better of you and you read it anyway? You just couldn't put it down? Well, I knew in my heart I should put the book down, but I was compelled to go to the first page just to find out when Pastor Chuck first began to write in this book.

A page toward the front caught my eye, it was dated approximately six years before and stated simply,

> *"This evening I received a phone call from the President of this medium sized congregation in greater Metropolitan Atlanta, GA. I talked to the President, George Harrelson, who informed me that the congregation had just completed a call meeting. At the meeting the voters voted unanimously to issue a call to the Pastorate of Shepherd of the Sheep Church Congregation of their suburb of Atlanta, GA."*

Because it was getting to the time, I was expecting the couple for counseling. I turned the pages until I was stopped at the next dated entry. The next entry described his trip to visit Shepherd of the Sheep Church.

> *"Helen and I arrived about 1:00 PM at Hartsfield Airport in Atlanta. George met us at the gate and walked us through the process of getting our luggage and leaving the airport. We stopped first to get a bite to eat and then proceeded to the church property."*
>
> *"My impression of the church building and grounds: We drove along the city street until we came to a driveway with a wooden sign announcing Shepherd of the Sheep Church. As we turned from the street onto the driveway, up the small grade through the tree limbs I caught a glimpse of the white church building."*
>
> *"The church sign was positioned very close to the driveway where you would turn to drive up to the church.*

The lettering on the sign was small and barely readable. These two factors made it almost impossible to read the sign if you were driving along the road. If you drive into the driveway, you could read the sign. Also, if you pull the car close to the street curb and park, you can get out, go over to the sign, and read the street address: 3069 Peachtree Summit Road, the times of the church services and the Pastor's name."

"We drove up the little hill through the trees and there before us was the church complex. From the road, all I could see was trees and some lawn. George told us the parking lot was at the rear of the church complex. The church has a front door, but it looks as if it is seldom if ever used, but there is the front door, the poured concrete steps are there leading from the ground level to the church door, the poured concrete slab on the ground is there in front of the steps and the grass of the lawn which surrounds the slab on three sides gives the impression that it is there only for show."

"George continued driving until we were at the rear of the Church buildings where he parked the car close to the back door. We entered the church through the back door, the one the Congregation uses to enter the church on Sunday or any other time there is a scheduled activity at the church. He led us down a short hall and opened the door labeled Pastor, invited us into the Pastor's office and motioned for us to sit in the upholstered chairs there."

"George asked Helen and me if we would like to take a tour of the facility. Helen decided to remain in the Pastor's office while George gave me a complete tour. She had found a current edition of Christian Times and decided that she wanted to catch up on her reading. He began with an in-depth tour of the buildings."

"The church plan is laid out in the shape of a capital T. The Sanctuary is one-half of the top of the T. The fellowship hall is the other half with a moveable wall connecting the Sanctuary to the Fellowship Hall able to be opened, so overflow seating can be accommodated with folding chairs in the Fellowship Hall. The Sanctuary pews can comfortably seat about two hundred twenty-five people. The pastor's office is at the Altar end of the Sanctuary. At the end of this hall is a door to the outside."

"The Educational wing, the equivalent of the upright of the T, is attached at the point where the Sanctuary and the fellowship hall come together. It has a hallway up the middle with bathrooms, classrooms and the church secretary's office doors opening into it. The classrooms are medium sized and set up with tables and chairs to hold fifteen or less Sunday school students. The largest classroom holds the adult Bible Class and doubles as the meeting room for some of the church boards and the Church Council. The church Secretary's office has a desk a chair for the church secretary, several folding chairs for visitors, file cabinets, a typewriter, a Gestetner mimeograph machine, a scanner to make stencils and a small church safe. The Sanctuary and fellowship hall are of concrete block construction on poured concrete slabs. The Educational wing is a combination of concrete block and wood walls constructed on a slab."

"George and I walked outside onto the parking lot. As we looked around, I am standing with my back to the building, could see the lot line on my left as it disappeared into the wooded area. To my right, all I could see was the wooded area next to the parking lot. He told me that the church owned four and one-half acres of land and this building and the church grounds currently occupied about

one and one-half acre. He led the way, and we began walking on a trail that led into the woods. This certainly is a nice chunk of land and there is no end in the ways it can be used to further God's kingdom. We began to talk about of past plans for the land. We began to dream of what could be, and how this could help grow the church. As we walked and talked together, I realized that the possibilities for furthering the work of the Lord with that much land available are awesome!"

"Back in the church building, Helen had finished reading the magazine and was ready to look around a little. Helen, George, and I did a walking tour of the facility so I could get a feeling from her about the buildings at a later time. George showed us the boardroom where the evening meeting with The Church Council was to be held. George took us out for an early supper and then drove us to the motel so Helen and I could relax and prepare for the meeting tonight."

"Back in the privacy or the motel room, I asked Helen for her assessment of the church property. She has a good eye for this and has attended a number of church growth seminars with me. She also takes a commonsense approach. The question she always asks is: 'What would an un-churched stranger think about the church and the people who belong to it when he or she walked in the door? Is the atmosphere inviting? Would they consider coming back?' Her assessment was to the point, 'the facility is not run down in any way but is not inviting. It needs to be dressed up and modernized. Special work is needed in the women's rest room to make that inviting.'"

As I sat there in his chair, reading about the first time he and I met, my memories flooded back. I had called him on the phone that Sunday when the congregation voted to send him the call. We had such a positive conversation that evening. The memories came back of me meeting him and his wife the first time at the airport.

As the people came off the plane, I had walked up to this distinguished looking man, dressed in the black suit with clerical collar, and introduced myself to him. When I called him by name I was corrected, as I wasn't talking to Pastor Charles Berg, I was talking to Father Robert Flanagan! I then speedily took out my pen and wrote on the back of an envelope I had in my sport coat pocket *'Shepherd of the Sheep Church'* and held it up for the people deplaning to see.

Eventually this average looking man, dressed in golf shirt and beige slacks, carrying a garment bag came up to me and introduced himself as Pastor Charles Berg. He then turned around and found Helen, who had not made it out of the plane as fast and introduced me to her. I never did tell him about my encounter with Father Robert Flanagan.

I remembered how with great pride I showed him around the church and grounds. How we had talked about what could be done with so much land. Maybe even about the dreams of church growth I had. I remember taking them to Denny's for an early supper and later going back and picking them up at the Red Roof Inn, near the church, to bring them back for the meeting with The Church Council.

I continued reading:

> *"Although she didn't want to come, I convinced Helen I needed her input as an independent observer at the meeting with The Church Council. George picked us up at 7:30 for the 8:00 p.m. meeting. I had not been briefed and therefore had no idea what this meeting was to be about. Were they going to grill me about my adherence to Holy Scripture, Church Law, or any liberal leanings I*

might have? Was I being set up? What were they looking for? Nothing like this has ever happened to me in any of my previous calls."

"We arrived a little early and the council members began to arrive one by one. The Church Council was made up of the Chairmen of the various church boards. I was there to be introduced to each member as he arrived, at least that seemed to be George's plan."

"The first council member to arrive was Harold Lee, the Vice President of the congregation. Next was Herbert Gross, the Treasurer, and Lois Grenbach, the Corporate Secretary, arrived. The Chairman of the Board of Evangelism, Howard Lemke, made it into the board-room one minute before the clock read 8:00. George hadn't gaveled the meeting to order yet and my wondering why came moments later when board Chairperson Emily Windsor from the Board of Social Ministry came huffing and puffing in. About 8:05 p. m., just after Emily finally got seated, Glen Ritch Chairman of the Board of Elders quietly tried to sneak in uttering a string of apologies for being late. Still, the meeting had not been gaveled to order and at about 8:11 the financial Secretary, David Arthur, arrived followed almost immediately by Ann Helgeson, Chairperson of the Board of Education. Then came the Chairman of the Board of Stewardship, Jack Lofton, and the Board of Youth Ministries, Joe Summers. Finally, the last two board Chairmen, Richard Nelson of the Trustees and Billy Jackson of Finance arrived. George gaveled the meeting to order at 8:25 p.m."

"The first thing he did was to formally introduce Helen and me to the council members. He then had each

board member stand and introduce themselves to us by giving name, board, occupation and family status."

"That makes five white collar people, two business owners, four blue collar workers, one home maker, and one retired person on the Council. An interesting mix, much different from the mix in the congregation I currently serve. These people are on the average much older than at my current congregation. This is interesting."

"After the introductions, George announced the purpose of this meeting. This meeting was for me to get to know each council member and ask them questions pertaining to the work they do for the church. His suggestions to the Chairmen were that they give a thumbnail sketch as to what the boards were doing, what plans each board had for future projects, and give a general indication of where the board was headed. To my relief, this was a meeting for my benefit, to help me assess the mood and current direction of the congregation."

This was all he had written about that first meeting. As I read his account, memories from that night came back to me. I had so wanted The Church Council to make a good impression on the pastor we had just called. It really upset me that that only four out of the thirteen people needed for that meeting arrived on time. I had suspected but not realized that out of all of the things discussed during that meeting, this was the one of the two things the called pastor would have noted.

When was the last time you listened to something you overheard and felt guilty about it? I was going through my second pangs of guilt that night when I finished reading those pages, yet *I still could not stop!* This was the book Pastor Chuck had been writing on when he was interrupted. If the interruption were non-violent, if it were voluntary, I was sure the reason could be alluded to from what was written somewhere near the end of his entries in this book. Then why was I reading these entries near the beginning?

I don't know, I can't say!

I looked out of the window and realized it was becoming early evening. I hadn't called Elizabeth and told her where I was. I checked my watch and watched the digital numbers change from 7:39:59 to 7:40:00. She expected me home by 5:30 and I got so involved in this that I didn't call her. By now, she was probably as worried about me as Helen was about Pastor Chuck. After all I was much older than Pastor Chuck.

Through the receiver, I heard the ringing of the phone at the other end of the line.

"Hello?" came Liz's voice.

"Hello, it is me," I said.

"Where are you? I have started to call around and nobody knows where you are! Are you okay?" she asked with concern in her voice.

"I'm fine, I'm at church. Pastor is missing, and I am trying to investigate," I told her.

"What do you mean Pastor is missing? I saw him just last night at the Voters Assembly Meeting," she answered.

I filled her in on the situation as I knew it. I told her I promised I would stay around until Pastor came back to meet with the couple he was counseling and come home after he got here. She thought that was a good plan.

It was a good plan.

THE WAITING TIME

I LOOKED AROUND THE OFFICE TO MAKE sure I had placed everything back in the exact order in which I had found them. After placing his diary and Bible on his desk in the positions I had found them, I sat for a few moments in the Pastor's chair looking at the reproduction of the painting of *Jesus Knocking at Heart's Door*. My thoughts wandered back to the pages I had just read from the beginning of the Pastor's diary.

I wondered what it would be like to be a pastor receiving a call to a distant congregation. I sold Insurance. I had chosen where to set up my office. I, as an independent agent, was free to choose the companies I wished to represent. I was in control, as much as any of us can be, of my life and my destiny.

On the other hand, a pastor is chosen by God, sent out from the Seminary on a call and has the opportunity to serve the same congregation for his whole productive life. Then a call comes from another congregation. It must take a lot of prayer and faith for a pastor to give up the comfort of the known to accept a call to the unknown. I sat there deep in thought for a long time until I heard a knocking at the back door of the church.

I looked at my watch and found that the time had slipped by rather fast while I had been deep in thought. It was 7:55 and the Pastor was not here yet. I got up from his chair, locked his office door before I left and made my way to the door where the knocking came from.

I met the young couple at the door and invited them into the building.

"I'm George Harrelson, President of the Shepherd of the Sheep Congregation," I said, introducing myself.

"I'm Henry Schoenfeldt and this is my fiancée, Ellen Morgan," Henry said as he made his introductions.

"Glad to meet you," I responded and led them to the Board Room.

We sat at the end of the table closest to the door on metal folding chairs with the two of them sitting in chairs across the table from me. I got to know them quite well while we awaited the Pastor's arrival. I hadn't noticed them at church and had never met them.

Henry began by telling me their story.

"We have been dating for about two years. We met at work. Ellen is in the Marketing department, and I am in Engineering. Ellen is a native of Seattle, Washington, and I grew up in Ohio, around Cleveland. I was a member of a church affiliated with Shepherd of the Sheep, and Ellen attended a church of another denomination," he explained.

"When we began to date, neither of us was attending church regularly, but, as things became more serious, we began to look around for a church where we could both feel comfortable. We visited Shepherd of the Sheep Congregation and found a church that fit," he continued.

At this point in the story, Ellen picked up the thread.

"We visited a number of churches and then we began to come here on a regular basis. I wanted us to go to the same church. I think if a family goes to the same church together, they might have less of a chance for divorce. We have been attending the second service now on a regular basis for six months. We are in his membership class," she explained.

Henry interrupted, "my membership is being handled by transfer and Ellen is joining by profession of faith. We decided to attend his membership class together."

Ellen then continued, "We will become members very soon now. We have asked Pastor Chuck to marry us. We have not chosen the date yet, but it will be soon."

I sensed it was time for me to make some kind of comment, "We are happy to have you join our congregation."

I looked at my watch. It indicated the time was now 8:20 and Pastor had still not arrived.

I looked across the table at those two bright young smiling faces and said, "Obviously, something has come up that has delayed Pastor Chuck, and it is doubtful that he will be here for the counseling session. I think the best thing for you to do is to go home and discuss the situation with Pastor after church on Sunday."

Henry looked at his watch, looked over to Ellen and said, "That is probably the best thing to do. Come on Ellen, let's go."

I walked with them to the door and said our goodbyes, then they were gone.

I went back to Pastor's office. First, I called home to update Liz. I told her it looked like I would be there for quite a while as Pastor hadn't come back for his marriage counseling session. I told her that it appeared we would now have to look at this as if Pastor Chuck had run into some kind of problem – was he kidnapped or worse.

I suggested to her that I thought it would be a good idea for me to stay at the church and establish a command center. Liz agreed with me and wanted to come to the church and help wherever she could. She decided she would fix us supper plates from the meal that was awaiting my arrival and bring them over at about 9:00 so we could eat together. I liked the idea and told her I would be waiting.

I dialed the phone again, this time to the parsonage.

The phone rang, "Hello, you have reached the Berg's."

"Hello, it is me George," I answered. "Pastor didn't arrive for his marriage counseling appointment."

There was a long silence at Helen's end of the phone and finally when she spoke, she uttered a faint, "Oh."

"Before I did anything, I wanted to talk to you. You know him best. I don't want to start searching for him if he is some place close and will turn up soon. On the other hand, if I wait and find he was in deep trouble, I don't want to have started too late. I really don't want to have this embarrass him." I explained.

"I know him, this is not like him, his car is there, he has always called me and told me when he was going to be late, and he missed an appointment! Something is really wrong!" she emphatically stated.

"I just don't want to jump the gun on this," I answered trying to sound reasonable.

"I know him! He always tells me what he is doing. I didn't hear by noon, but I held off, I only called you when I began to worry. Now that he has missed his appointment… you have to do something! This is the first time anything like this has ever happened!" she continued.

By this time, Helen's voice sounded pretty frantic over the phone.

"Helen, I am going to stay here at the church and coordinate everything from here. You are welcome to come here and join me if it will help you. Liz will be her soon," I answered.

Her answer was immediate, "I will be there as soon as I get the kids organized."

"Good, I will be waiting for you. In the meantime, I will get as many Elders involved as possible," I reassured her.

"Thank you, George. Goodbye," she responded.

"Goodbye," I answered and hung up.

I sat there in Pastor's chair in his office and tried to gather my thoughts. I needed to call the Chairman of the Board of Elders, but what would I say to him? Maybe Pastor is missing? Or we can't find Pastor, or have you seen Pastor this evening? How much of my concern will follow my voice through the phone line to him? Finally, I picked up the receiver and began to dial the phone number of Paul Hessman, Head Elder.

The Phone rang five times and I almost thought Paul wasn't home before it was answered.

"Hi, Hessman's," a male voice said.

"Hello, is Paul there?" I asked.

"Uh-huh, I'll get him," came the reply.

Apparently, one of his sons had answered and I waited until Paul's familiar voice came on the line.

"Can I help you?" he asked.

"Hello Paul, this is George. We have a little problem here at the church. Pa…" I hesitated for a moment and was interrupted by Paul.

"What kind of a problem?" Paul asked.

"I don't really know how to describe it, Paul, but Pastor has been missing for most of the day. Helen and I are really worried about him. We have to do something. Can you get the Elders together and meet here at church by 9:45?" I asked.

"I'll get together as many as I can. What should I tell them?" he asked.

"Tell them it is an emergency. We can't find Pastor Chuck and we need to discuss what steps we should take to locate him and to cover the needs of the church in the meantime. Oh, and tell them I have invited Helen also," I answered.

"Will do," was all he said and hung up the phone.

I sat in the pastor's office just trying to plan what we would have to do? What is appropriate to do? Where could Pastor Chuck have gone? I looked at the open Bible lying on his Diary and wondered if the circled chapter and the underlined verses had anything to do with where he is.

I looked at my watch and noted that it was just 9:13 p.m. Just as I began to wonder where Liz was with the evening meal she had promised, I heard her at the door. I got up from the pastor's desk and headed to the boardroom to meet her. It would have been warmer and cozier to have eaten in Pastor Chuck's office, but I would have had to clear away papers on his desk to place the plates and as it was, I didn't want to really touch anything on his desk.

Liz placed a large cloth on top of the table in the boardroom and placed the plates of food on the cloth. She uncovered the plates and beheld, what a meal. There were nuked slices of meatloaf, whipped up instant potatoes, sliced carrots, and to top that off there was a thermos bottle of scalding hot coffee. We sat down and I led us in the table prayer. Until I dug in and began to feel the warmth of the food in my stomach, I had not been aware of the hunger I must have had but been too worked up to have felt.

We were about half through with the meal when Helen came into the boardroom. She appeared tired and it was obvious that she had been crying. Liz immediately got up from the table, went up to her, and gave her a big hug. That unleashed another round of tears. The two of them went down the hall to the women's rest room and I was left alone to finish my meal.

It was about ten minutes later when they both came back. We talked for a few minutes while Liz finished what she wanted of her meal. I suggested we adjourn to the Pastor's office and have Helen look around for any clue to what might have gotten him out of his office.

THE ELDERS GATHER

WE WERE IN PASTOR'S OFFICE WHEN PAUL arrived. Helen had looked around but had seen nothing that would help us to find Pastor. We went back to the boardroom to await the arrival of more Elders. Shortly a somber looking Paul came hurriedly into the boardroom.

"I could only get in touch with half of the Elders," Paul reported. "Howard Lemke said he would be right over, Glen Rich will come, Henry Paulson promised to be here, Henry Farmer and Bill Stricker both said they might be a little late. I left messages for the rest of them. I don't know if any of the rest of them will make it."

Glen Rich and Henry Paulsen arrived soon after Paul spoke. Bill Stricker and Henry Farmer followed them a couple minutes later. I decided not to start the meeting until Howard arrived. As we waited on Howard, the others were standing around the room full of questions, it was difficult to answer each of the Elder's individual questions.

In desperation I said, "Would everyone please find a spot and sit at the table. I will try to answer as many of your questions as soon as Howard gets here. In the meantime, I would ask that we all say a silent prayer for the safety of Pastor Chuck."

In the quiet that followed you could hear a pin drop.

The silence was broken when Howard arrived exclaiming, "I got here as fast as I could!"

"Take a seat Howard." I commanded. "Paul, as this is an Elders' meeting would you gavel this meeting to order?" I asked.

Paul opened, "will this meeting please come to order? Let us pray."

We all bowed our heads and Paul said a prayer. Paul then turned the meeting over to me.

"Now, we are gathered here because pastor seems to be missing. Helen, would you tell us what you can about this?" I asked.

Helen described in detail the events from the time Pastor called home after the meeting last night to the lack of communication with him to this present time. She expressed the concern she had for his health and why she called me to check on him. The fact that his car is here, and he missed his counseling session has her more than just worried.

"Thank you, Helen, for giving us what information you have," I paused for a moment to think then continued, "Pastor Chuck's absence is something we must address. The question is: What action should we take? I have been mulling this over in my mind since about 7:30. Pastor works closely with the Elders and in effect reports to them, I decided that we as a group should work out a plan to handle this situation. We can take our plan to the Church Council if we must. Paul, I would like to turn the meeting over to you. Helen and Liz, you are welcome to join in as part of this Elders' meeting."

Paul took the floor, "Gentlemen, first I would like to define the problem in greater detail. Howard, you are closest to the white board, would you start writing what we know in one column?"

Howard, a schoolteacher with extensive white board experience, got up and went over to the white board and picked up a marker ready to make a list.

Paul looked over the table and asked, "Henry, would you please take notes?"

Henry got up, went over to a shelf, picked up some paper and a pen, and headed back to his seat at the table. Henry Farmer was a clothing store Manager over at the mall and usually took very precise notes.

"Ok, let's get to work!" Paul commanded.

At that moment, Lester Smith, an older retired man, came through the open door and asked, "What's happening? I made it here as fast as I could as soon as I got your message. Why the urgent phone call, Paul?"

Paul looked around the table at the other Elders and then answered Lester, "Pastor is missing, we are discussing what to do. I'll fill you in on any details you missed later. Now, does anyone have any suggestions?"

"It is after 10:00, and we haven't even got started. I have to get up early to get to work. Let's get going. This isn't an Engineering project," interrupted Henry Paulson a factory worker at the GM Doraville Plant.

"Okay, what do we know?" questioned Paul.

"Helen laid it out rather plain. Pastor is missing!" I responded.

"The question is what should we do about it?" questioned Bill, the owner of a plumbing business.

"I think we should call the police and alert them to the fact that our Pastor is missing?" Henry suggested.

"I agree with Henry, we should call the Police," stated Glen, the car salesman in the group.

"Howard, write that on the board," commanded Paul.

"Would it do any good to get in our cars and try to look for him?" questioned Lester.

"Where would we look?" asked Henry.

"Well, we got to do something!" Lester replied.

"The question is what do we want to do? Do we want to publicize the fact that Pastor is missing? What if we go to the police and he shows up right away? Wouldn't that be an embarrassment to him? Have we thought this through enough? Let's follow Paul's plan and write what we know up on the board," suggested Bill.

"Yah, let's get this organized," Howard agreed.

"We have to think this through." Paul stated, "Howard get ready, Pastor was here last night at 10:00. What time did he call you, Helen?" Paul asked as he took back command of the meeting.

"He called right at 10:30 because I was watching the commercial at the end of the 10:00 news," Helen stated.

"What exactly did he say when he called?" asked Paul.

"He called and said that the meeting was over, it was a little rougher than he had expected, he was tired, had something he needed to do and might spend the night on the couch." She stated.

"Is this something he usually does?"

"No, he only stays over Saturday night if he has had a hard time preparing his sermon. Then he stays over at church. He then sleeps on Sunday afternoon when he gets home." Helen explained.

"Didn't you think it was odd that he decided to stay?" I asked.

"Yes, but he sounded so tired. He has been so tired lately. That's why I was so concerned about his health and his heart. He has been under so much stress lately," Helen stated in a concerned voice.

I continued, "so your biggest concern is his health."

"I want to know he is safe!" she replied.

"When did you begin to worry?" I continued to question her, and Howard continued to make notes on the board.

"When he didn't come home for breakfast and didn't call. I didn't want to bother him if he was busy, and I didn't want him to think I was worried. When he didn't come home for lunch was when I started to phone the church. When I didn't get him there, I called you to go check on him."

Paul took over again, "We will assume he went missing sometime in the morning then. George, you got here sometime after 3:00 and found his car here and he was nowhere around the premises, right?"

"Right," I replied.

Paul continued, "did you look in his office for any clues as to what he was thinking or where he had gone?"

"I found a journal entry, but it was not complete and was of no help. Later this evening, Helen and I both looked around in the office and still couldn't find anything," I answered.

"Then this is what we know," Paul pointed out.

1.   "We will assume he disappeared in the mid-morning."
2.   "He left no notes or indication he was leaving nor any indication of where he might be going."
3.   "He has missed breakfast, lunch, and dinner."
4.   "He missed his 8:00 p.m. appointment."
5.   Whatever he did or wherever he went to, he didn't take his car," Paul stated as Howard wrote the points on the board.

Paul continued, "Now, we need to list the concerns we have about him. We have been sitting here a long time. I think it would be good to get up and stretch. Is there any coffee?"

We took a fifteen-minute break while Liz made coffee. The rest of us stood around in little groups and discussed the situation and what we could do about it. At 11:30, I gaveled them back to the table.

"Let's list our concerns." I suggested.

Howard approached the board ready to write.

Paul started it off,

"1. Concerns about Pastor's health, 2. Concerns that someone had come by the church and forced him to go with him, 3. He had decided to go for a walk and been accosted and hurt. Does anyone else have any ideas to put on the board?"

Everyone was silent.

"Then, what is the best action for us to take tonight?" Paul asked.

Henry Paulsen raised his hand and when Paul nodded to him, he spoke, "I think the best thing to do is to call the police. They would know if anyone matching Pastor's description has been found."

Glen spoke up, "I agree with Henry. It would be best if the police could keep an eye out for him."

Several others then chimed in their agreement, and it was settled. Paul would use Glen's notes and file a missing person's report with the police.

"I will call around to the local hospitals to check on any unusual admissions," added Paul.

"I'll spend the night here, so we have a central coordination point to work from. I will camp out in Pastor's office on the couch. Is there a motion to adjourn this meeting?" I asked.

"I so move," said Howard.

"I second," Bill announced.

"All in favor rise and we will close with The Lord's Prayer." I responded.

We said the prayer, and everyone left to go home. I asked Helen if she needed help and she said she was all right now. Liz gave her a hug and told her she would go home with her to help where she could. The church was now empty as I headed for Pastor's office.

PASTOR'S ACCEPTANCE

I sat in Pastor's chair facing his desk, and in front of me, under the Bible, was his diary. I didn't feel sleepy. The meetings were over. I felt relief that we were doing something. I was holding down the fort. This was the most comfortable place for me to spend the night.

I kept looking at the Bible and the diary that were open in front of me. I knew I really shouldn't, but I felt the excitement of doing something I probably shouldn't do. It was as though I was compelled to move the Bible and look again at the Diary. I opened it and found the entry I had read earlier. The next entry in Pastor Chuck's diary was two weeks later.

> *"Today at the Board of Elders meeting Josh Blume, the head elder, called me aside after the meeting ended. He told me he noticed I am looking exhausted, and he asked how my consideration of the call is going. Josh has been my rock and is always there when I need someone to open up to. His father spent his whole life as the pastor of a large old metropolitan German Speaking Church. Josh learned a lot growing up in the parsonage. Tonight, he has read me right again. He has put his finger on the stress I have*

from this call. He said if I wanted to talk, he would listen. We sat in the board room, and I began to share my hopes, reservations, and fears with him."

"I like it here! I am comfortable here! I am happy here! I love the people here! I am not looking forward to change. I wasn't looking for a call. Then, why is this call eating at me so? Why does it always come back to haunt me?"

"I am praying constantly about this, and I keep making up my mind only to feel pressure to reread the call. One day, I set it aside and am ready to decline it. That night I can't sleep. I pray again and after maybe a day I decide to take it. I look around the church and all the love the congregation has shown me and change my mind. For the past two weeks, I have just gone back and forth."

"Josh looked straight at me. 'He said Chuck,' he didn't say Pastor Chuck, 'he said Chuck,' and looked at me while I reacted to what he said."

"He continued talking, 'I called you Chuck because right now I want to talk to you as a fellow Christian. I want to put aside our relationship. I want to pass on to you some of the experience of my long years of being a Christian. I have known many pastors in my life and each one has had to look a call in the eyes and make a choice. I have had the opportunity to counsel a number of them. The advice I have given is ask yourself these questions:

1. *Will I have to break any commitments to any members by accepting this call?*

2. *Are there any projects that will be hurt by my leaving at this time?*

3. *Is the congregation able to function in the interim after I leave?*

4. *Is it time for me to leave to further the spiritual growth of the congregation?*
5. *Am I too comfortable here and need to move for the sake of my spiritual growth?*
    Your answer to these questions should give you some guidance in how to answer the call.'"

That was the last entry for about a week and a half. The next entry was more upbeat. Pastor Chuck wrote,

"Today after my morning prayers, I decided to look at the call papers one more time and try to digest what the congregation at Shepherd of the Sheep Church is asking of me in this call. There is this area describing the goals and dreams of the congregation. I read them over again and compared them to the notes I had from my visit with the Church Council. It became obvious that the call was for someone that could be both the spiritual leader to help them grow in faith and the evangelistic leader to lead them in bringing the Word of God into the community. Suddenly this all made sense. I had fulfilled that role with my current congregation, and we were at a plateau. They needed someone new to lead them to a new level. Shepherd of the Sheep Church congregation needed me to fill that role with them. There it was in the call document and my notes from the meeting. They had land, but it was not being used to further God's Kingdom. They needed programs to connect to the community, ways to use the facility God had given them, programs for Education, Evangelistic Outreach, and Social Ministry."

That was the end of his notes on that page. I decided it was at that point when he had made his decision to accept the call. I received the signed call documents indicating his acceptance in mid-April stating he would be moving at the beginning of June and would preach his first sermon the second Sunday in June.

Again, I remembered what it had been like. Immediately when I had received the letter, I called a Council meeting to make preparations for the move. We decided to place him on the payroll as of June first. We had to find him a suitable house. It was decided to fly him and his wife down to go house hunting for several days at the end of April so the house would be ready to move into on June first.

The House hunting was the first challenge. They were coming from a more rural market to a Metropolitan area. The house they were selling was double the size of the house they could buy near the church for the same money. Pastor wanted to live near the church in that community, but this was not going to be possible. We found an affordable house they liked in a community about eighteen miles away.

His house that he was selling was in walking distance of the church and they were a one car family. Now, they were going to become a two-car family. The good thing was that Helen fell in love with the house, and the school system they would be a part of was highly ranked.

Richard Nelson, the chairman of the Board of Trustees, was up to his neck in the details of the move. It was up to him to find the moving company and make those arrangements. On the other hand, Herbert Gross, the Treasurer, was pulling his hair out and he didn't have much hair he could lose. Trying to move funds around to pay the moving expenses and keep the cash flow was the real trick.

Richard had obtained quotes from all the moving companies he could find, but he rejected the lowest bid. It was rejected because of what he had heard when he checked the company out. The next bid was double what had been budgeted. Three weeks of prayer, and a very well-constructed letter of appeal from Billy Jackson, Chairman of the Board of Finance, brought into the collection plate more than enough to pay for the move. The extra was given to Helen to buy drapes and other things for the new house.

The Ladies Aid Society, The Board of Education, and the Board of Elders worked to put together the welcoming activities for Pastor and his family. The eight weeks from the time he accepted the call until the time he preached his first sermon was a buzz of activity.

I turned the page of his diary and read the next entry. There was excitement in the words he had written.

> *"I know this move is the right one. Shepherd of the Sheep Church congregation is where I belong! The Demographics are right for church growth. The land is there. I believe I have the training. The Lord is making the way easy. We had the house listed for five days and someone put a contract on it for what we were asking! Helen loves the new house and even the children are excited about moving to the Greater Atlanta area. The congregation has taken care of arranging the move and everything is all set. I am installed the first Sunday in June and I preach my first sermon second Sunday in June."*

There was a space and then the next entry,

> *"Last night, the Congregation had a farewell Potluck Dinner for us. We knew it was going to happen and we thought it would be held at church, but as the time for the dinner to start approached only a few people arrived at church. I got a little discouraged as it didn't seem like anyone was coming. About fifteen minutes before it was to happen, the President came to the door and invited us to follow him in his car. We followed him to the High School Gym. There were so many people from the church and the town wanting to say goodbye that they had to rent a bigger*

place! We must have had half the town there. Even Father
O'Donald stood up to make a few remarks. He opined that
my leaving should make his job a whole lot easier."

That was all that was on that page. When I turned the page, he had begun to make notes about Shepherd of the Sheep Church.

A JOYOUS ARRIVAL

I HAD BEEN READING FOR A WHILE and decided to get up and check out the coffee supply. I should be considering lying down on the couch and catching a little shuteye, that would be the prudent thing to do. If the phone rang, I would wake up and be able to coordinate whatever I could. Instead, I headed for the coffee pot and, *eureka*, there was still some leftover from the earlier meeting. After all, I wanted to continue reading in the Pastor's Diary. *I was hooked!*

The next entries were short. The first was in was in mid-June, only a paragraph.

> *"We are moved in, and I have finished my first Sermon. My installation went well. The congregation made it a great celebration. I was overwhelmed by the size of the crowd. I have never seen so many people come to an installation."*
>
> *"I had the chance to spend some time with the president of my new district and several of the pastors from the surrounding churches. I believe I was led here to expand God's Kingdom. I am where I belong."*

How I remember that Installation! We tried to '*impress*' him and make him feel at home at the same time. The visiting pastor that preached that day had a crowd for the eight-o-clock service which was unusual. Attendance at the nine-fifteen Sunday school was good. The ten-thirty service was packed.

We sure had a lot of visitors! During Sunday school hour, we had to assign some of the men to the parking lot to decide where to park all the cars. We had to start parking them on the grass in front of the church.

The installation festivities began at 4:00 p.m. that Sunday. With the turnout we had for the morning services in expectation of an overflow crowd for this service we set up all the chairs we had in the fellowship hall for overflow seating and opened the divider at the back of the sanctuary. We experienced an overflow crowd. We again needed help with the parking lot.

We had scheduled it late in the day so that more pastors from the surrounding area could come. The Congregation was settled in the pews and the folding chairs in the Fellowship Hall. All was ready for the Processional. The Crucifer led the way followed by two banner bearers. Behind them came the District President, the visiting Pastors, Pastor Chuck, the Head Elder and Myself.

The service began with a hymn sung by the Choir and some readings. The Words of Installation were pronounced by the District President and that part of the service was concluded by the laying of hands-on pastor from all the visiting pastors and the two of us from the congregation. One of the visiting pastors conducted the service, another gave a homily, another led us in prayer, and we sang a final hymn. The service ended with the procession of the clergy out of the sanctuary.

Thirty minutes later, the Fellowship Hall was cleared, tables were set up, and we were all lined up to partake of one of the best Potluck dinners we ever had. I was fortunate enough to have given the welcoming speech at the beginning of the meal. We all lined up to fill our plates and find a place to eat. We had not expected this large of a turnout so there were people eating all over the church. *Such enthusiasm!*

The next entry was short and mentioned about him getting to know the various boards. He was happy that the boards were so well organized. He had attended his first voter's assembly meeting, the one for the third quarter. He was happy that the meeting went well.

The next entry was in the last week of September,

> "I have finally found out the meaning for the term "Falcon Mass" that I kept over hearing. It accounts for the uptick in first service attendance I have been noticing. It has to do with the Atlanta Falcons football season. It appears that those fans without season tickets make fun of those who do. Those that have season tickets come to first service to get a head start to go to the stadium. Those who don't have season tickets kid those who go to the first service as attending "Falcon Mass". What a name for first service!"
>
> "I have assessed the situation, and this is the list of changes I believe are needed to begin growing the church. To get this started, these are needed need to be presented at the next Church Council Meeting. 1. The trees in front of the church need to be trimmed so the church can be seen from the road, 2. The parking lot needs to be expanded, 3. The church sign must be able to be read by someone in a car driving past the property."

It was toward the end of that week that Pastor asked me to come over to the church after work and 'plan' with him. I drove over and parked next to his car by the side of the church. Pastor met me as I came in the side door.

"Hi George, let's go and get a cup of coffee and take a look at some of the things we need to do to make this place a friendlier place to visitors."

I followed him to the coffee pot in the secretary's office and got a cup of coffee to which I added cream and quite a bit of sugar. I noticed that he took his black.

"Let's go back to my office. I want to go over with you some things I have been praying about, some things I am going to present to Council. I want to get your feedback."

I sipped my coffee so I wouldn't spill any on the floor on the way back to his office and followed him in. He sat on the visitor's chair and motioned to me to sit on the couch. I think he wanted this to be an informal chat and he wanted us to be as comfortable as possible.

He opened the conversation by saying, "we want to spread the Gospel from the confines of this campus out into the surrounding area. We need to begin by making our campus more visible to people passing through our neighborhood."

He paused and looked at me. This was the first time I had heard him refer to the church facility as a campus. I must have had a stunned look on my face or something.

Then he continued, "To make this campus more inviting we have to do something about that sign."

I interrupted, "Richard Nelson had the sign painter paint your name on the sign, did he not place it right?" I thought we got that done rather quickly.

"That's not the problem with the sign," Pastor Chuck pointed out. "It makes no difference whose name is on that sign when you can't read it from a car going thirty-five miles an hour from the road. We have to get a larger sign!"

I thought for a moment before answering him.

"The congregation discussed a new sign a year ago. At that time, it would have cost over $5,000. The Church Council presented this to the Voter's Assembly. It wasn't in the budget and the expenditure was eventually tabled," I defensibly responded.

"It needs to be addressed again then," he continued.

"Next, we need to look at the visibility of the church from the street. If you notice when you drive by and look up the slight hill to the church, you see mostly tree branches, grass, and pine needles. The only part of the church building you see is the foundation, which is mostly covered up by the bushes planted around the foundation. The driveway isn't well marked either. If you don't know where it is, you might drive by and never realize the church is there. I would like to see what it looks like with the trees gone. It is a pretty enough building to make the statement Christ is here!" he stated.

I knew he was right. Richard Nelson and I had made the same observation on a number of occasions to only to be voted down.

"I'll see what I can do," was my answer.

And he continued, "the parking lot, something must be done about the parking. Have you noticed how fast the paved part becomes full? I watched several women in high heels and open toed shoes walk across the grass on their way to paved section. It didn't look comfortable, and the grass was dry. What happens if it is raining or there is a lot of dew on the grass? Do they stay home? Come with me. We will drive around town and look at parking places that serve businesses."

He got up from his chair and I followed him out the side door of the church to his car. Being the last one out, I locked the door behind me. I got into his car, and he drove me to the back parking lot. We counted marked parking places.

"There are twenty-two. People also park on the driveway leading up to the church and one side of the car is on the pavement," I defensively stated.

"So, that gives us twelve more cars. That is thirty-four cars that have access to paving or at least some paving. If you use an average of four persons per car, that gives us a hundred and thirty-two people that can come from our parking lot. Of course, the overflow from the grass makes up the other fifty-five people we have for our average attendance of one hundred eighty-seven souls for Second Service."

He then drove me to several of the churches in the immediate area. We counted parking spaces. They all had paved parking for around one hundred cars. We counted the parking spaces in the local McDonalds. There were forty parking spaces there, seven more than we had. I was silent on the ride back to the church. He had made his point.

Pastor Chuck broke the silence, "George, we have to become more aggressive in how we show ourselves to the Community if we are going to get God's word out into the community. I am going to bring these three points up in my report to the Church Council. I want your support on these. Are you with me?"

"Yes, I will support your position and talk it up at the meeting," I replied.

"Thank you for your support. It is a little late so I will drop you at your car and head for home." He said as he pulled into the parking spot next to my car.

I got out of his car and said, "have a good night," as I opened the door of my car.

"Same to you," he yelled back as he drove out the driveway toward the road.

Now, here I sat at his desk for a moment to bring my thoughts back to tonight's or more accurately this morning's situation. I looked back at his diary. I began to read his next entry. This was written after the Church Council meeting. There are times when it is better not to know what people sometimes think of you. This was one of those times.

Pastor had had written,

> *"I have survived my first list of changes presented at the Church Council Meeting. The president George Harrelson called the meeting to order. Glen Rich (Chairman of the Board of Elders) led us in an opening prayer and led us in an opening devotion."*

"I gave my first report on some of the things I had observed since coming here. This was just general observations. I made no proposals at this point. I decided to save them for the new business section of the agenda."

As I remember it, the council listened to the reports from the various board members and took care of the mundane problems that affect all churches in short order. Old Business was brought forward and handled. Billy Jackson, Board of Finance, brought up the program I had discussed with Jeff Gage, Stewardship and Herb Gross, Treasurer for the upcoming Stewardship drive. Nobody made any comments. Then it was time for new business.

Pastor Chuck led off, "George and I met last Thursday to discuss some of the observations I have made about ways to make this a friendlier place for people who come to visit. I think you all agree that if our congregation is to grow in this community, we have to be seen. We have to become a visible active part of our community. These are the three things I mentioned to George in our meeting. 1. We must be visible from the highway which would mean taking down and trimming back some of the trees in front of the church, 2. The church sign should be readable to anyone driving by the driveway going thirty-five miles per hour, and 3. There should be ample room in our paved section of our parking lot to make it easier to park on a paved spot."

I looked around the room to see how these proposals were met. Several of the board members looked nervous. A couple looked shocked.

Finally, Richard Nelson, head of the Board of Trustees, spoke, "I have wondered about these things and if you remember I brought up the parking lot situation last year when we had all of that wet weather. Nothing ever happened though."

Billy Jackson, head of the Board of Finance, also spoke, "If you remember, we got quotes and they were high. We didn't have any extra money at that time and the project was tabled."

The discussion went on and on over the sign and the trees. Finally, Hebert Gross moved that a committee be formed to look into these three issues and report back to the council before the next voters meeting. Howard Lemke, head of the Evangelism Board, seconded the motion, and all voted for it.

I continued reading. Pastor Chuck was positive that with a lot of prayer and a little discussion these simple things can be accomplished. That was the last entry on the page.

GETTING THINGS MOVING

I SET THE DIARY ASIDE AND RESTED for a moment from reading. I was thinking that I really should be getting some sleep. Everyone else had a job to do. I chose to sit around here to have a central coordination point for everyone to check in with. I could have easily done this from home, but the church seemed the best place for everyone to call when they found out something.

There was pastor's couch where I could lay down and catch some sleep. I looked at it and considered lying there, but really was I that sleepy? Actually, no. I guess in all of the excitement, my adrenaline rush had not worn off yet. Or was it that my curiosity to find out what else was in that diary that kept me awake. And yet, I felt that reading more of that diary was impinging on Pastor's privacy and the guilt from doing that weighed heavily on my mind.

I looked again at the open Bible, Chapter 4 in Mark, and the verses he had underlined. Did they have any bearing on the last sentences he had written on the last page of his diary? I thought about this for a while. I was tired but didn't feel as though I could actually sleep. I looked at the diary again. If I read further, could that lead me to think of what Pastor Chuck was thinking? Out of curiosity, I picked up the diary turned the page and found the next entry he made.

This entry was on the progress he was making with the Board of Finance on his thoughts on what the budget should look like. The youth program he was proposing was gaining support from George Michaelson, head of the Youth Ministries Board. Howard Lemke and the Board of Evangelism were working with him on outreach ideas he had. All in all, he was very enthusiastic as to the way things were going.

I scanned a few more pages and thought back to what he had written. Pastor Chuck and I had talked about how the boards had stepped up to function during the year and a half that Shepherd of the Sheep was without a pastor. Head Elder, Glen Rich, and I had impressed on the chairmen of each of the boards how important it was to keep the church moving forward during the vacancy.

They all had worked hard to keep things going. Because of all the work they did, the only members we lost were those who moved away, and we had actually gained some families who had been attending because of the youth programs we had, and they had indicated they would join as soon as we got a new pastor. We also wanted to look good to any pastor we were to call. We didn't want to have a pastor we called look at us in a negative light. We wanted to show him an ongoing family of faith who needed him as our leader.

As I was turning the pages, I came to Pastor's description of the October Council Meeting.

> "Tonight, the council meeting went well. Our Stewardship campaign is going well. George Michaelson is doing great things with the youth program. The only problem I am having is with the Board of Trustees. Richard Nelson hasn't moved forward yet with the committee to address the church sign, the visibility, or the parking lot. He didn't mention it in his Trustee's report although it was an item on the Agenda under Old Business. I will have to meet with George Harrelson to see what exactly the hold is up."

As I read that paragraph, I thought back to that time. I remember Pastor had made a point at that meeting that although the committee was listed under Old Business on the Agenda, he had not met with the committee if it had met and these items were very important for the upcoming Christmas season.

I had appointed a committee to be chaired by Richard. I had left it up to Richard to call the group together to look at the sign again, to do something about the trees, and to look at the parking lot again. The fact that he hadn't done anything yet probably was my fault for not pushing him. Anyway, I talked to him after the meeting.

He works for the pipeline company that has the tank farm in Doraville. His excuse was that this was fall and he was working a lot of overtime with the new winter gasoline coming in through the pipeline and anyway the report to Voter's Assembly wasn't until December. He thought he still had time.

We talked and decided that the least he could do was to see if the Trustee's budget had enough money left in it to hire a tree company to come in and at least trim the low hanging branches on the trees in the front of the church high enough so the church could be seen from the road. We agreed to call a meeting within the next week to meet with the pastor to get his input for a quote on a new sign, and his ideas on an addition to the parking lot.

Richard called a meeting and put his committee to work. He knew somebody who would trim up the trees in front of the church for a price low enough that he didn't have to get councils approval to have it done. The committee put forward, with Pastor's help, specifications for a quote on the sign. The committee also put forward a specification for expanding the parking lot.

The next entry was after the November Council meeting.

"Met with Emily Windsor and the Board of Social Ministry about what we could do special for Christmas. Met Ann

Helgeson, head of the Board of Education, and planned the Christmas Pageant. Glen Rich and the Elders are doing a good job. Richard Nelson had the trees trimmed in the front of the church. Wish he could have had some of them removed, but at least you can see the front door now and up to the roof eves. He still hasn't gotten the quotes back for the sign and the parking lot. I brought up the work Howard Lemke and I have been doing, researching avenues for the Board of Evangelism for his report to the Church Council. All else seems to be going well."

Reading his entry from six years ago brought back a flood of memories. The entry was a short entry and I remember the meeting went well. Before the meeting, he and I talked about the trees in front of the church. The trimming had made the building more visible from the highway, but the building didn't stand out. In his mind, he wanted the beauty of the church building to catch the eye, to stand out, and to look inviting to the motorist driving by at thirty-five miles an hour. His idea was that to foster growth, we must be part of the community! As it was in his mind, we were set apart from the community by how we presented ourselves.

He also told me about a project that he and Howard Lemke were working on. It was a way for us to be recognized in the greater community on a quarterly basis. It was a newspaper. A Christian company in Huntsville, Alabama printed a quarterly newspaper with all kinds of positive informational articles on all kinds of things. It also had a section where the pastor has space to give a message. The sponsoring congregation would send this paper to all of the homes in a specific city or community.

This in effect would be Shepherd of the Sheep Church's Quarterly News Paper. When he got through explaining the idea to me, I was impressed. He then produced an issue of the paper being used by another church in an adjoining area. The paper was about six pages and was placed in every mailbox in the designated area. The bulk mail postage cost for 10,000 came to $100.00. The cost of the paper was $0.11 a copy or about $900.00 a quarter which included the postage.

The November Church council meeting was called to order. I really don't remember all the individual board reports, but the boards had been busy. I remember things were going along quite well. Pastor Chuck gave his report, more a sermon than a report, but he gave his report.

In his report he stressed the importance of growing the church in the community where it is located. He called it his Mission Field. He pointed out that the latest surveys of communities the size of ours indicated that 50% of the people living in the community were un-churched. He also noted that 50% of our members live in the four-mile radius of the church and we have several members that live over twenty miles away. He noted we have a fertile field for Mission work.

The one board report I remember vividly was Richard Nelson's. In his report he mentioned that the committee had gone out for quotes for the sign and the parking lot, but he had not heard back yet. Howard Lemke gave an informational report on something the council members need to think about. A report on a Shepherd of the Sheep Church News Paper.

I skipped over reading the next entries which were routine notes about meetings with the various boards. Nothing about them brought up other memories, so I went to the next entry that concerned me. It was the December Church Council.

"*What is wrong with me?*" Pastor Chuck wrote.

> "*Haven't they heard a word I've said? I have told them of the great opportunity we have for Mission right here in our own community and they aren't listening! I have prayed over this, and I have this vision about where this congregation should go. Yet, except for Howard and*

George, it seems as though what I've said just goes past their ears. At least Richard has done something about the parking lot and the sign. We will see what happens at the congregational meeting."

"Jeff Gage's report on the pledge drive for stewardship was not what I had expected. Only 73% of the families in the congregation made pledges. I found out that this was not unusual. Billy Jackson explained to me after the meeting that when they put the budget together, they use the pledges as the start and then base the rest on the statistical historical giving that comes in from the plate offering. A budget based on faith."

"I was approached by a prospective new member family Sunday. Walter Stanke with his family has been visiting the past few Sundays. He talked to me about joining the church through transfer. He is the son of a pastor of an affiliated congregation in the Mid-west. With his background, he and his family could be a great asset to our congregation. I told him we are starting a new-members class in January. I invited him to come. He is new to the area, a corporate transfer."

I thought for a while about what I could remember from that Church Council meeting in December. I thought at the time that the council meeting went pretty well. The council had a budget to present to the congregation at the December meeting and Pastor, with Howard, had brought up the plan for outreach. That idea of a newspaper sponsored by the congregation was debated heavily during the meeting though. To some council members, it seemed like a bold move and the question was are we ready for such a move. To others, it was an expense we really didn't need, as we were doing pretty well as it was.

In the end though, it was placed on the agenda to be brought up in front of the voters at the December meeting. It was interesting his mentioning Walter Stanke. He had been so excited about Walter's background and what experiences he could bring to the congregation. If only he had known, then what trouble that new member would bring! If only! But the next entry caught my eye, and I turned the page.

POLITICAL REALITIES OF THE CHURCH

WHAT CAUGHT MY EYE ON THE NEXT page was the doodle at the top of the page. It was not a very large doodle, and I really don't know how to describe it other than it kind of looked like a finger with droplets of *something* dripping from it. If it was supposed to be a finger, it appeared that the fingernail had been the source of the droplets. Actually, it reminded me of the time I hit my finger really hard with a hammer and got blood all over my shirt.

Under it, Pastor Chuck had only written "*PRAY!*"

I continued reading,

> "*If this is an example of what the Annual Voters Assembly Meeting is going to be like, I will need all the prayers I can get. The reelection of the officers to the various boards took place without a problem. The board reports showcasing what had been accomplished this year went smoothly. Overall, it showed progress in many areas.*"
>
> "*Then Billy Jackson and the Board of Finance presented the operating budget for next year. Everything in*

the budget was questioned. After about 20 minutes of discussion, the motion was made to move the adoption of the budget until after new business was discussed as some of the things listed in new business could have an impact on the budget. The motion was seconded and passed. The old Business was a routine wrap up of what the boards reported. Then it came to the New Business."

"The first item in New Business was the church sign. Richard Nelson made a very good case for a new sign. George Harrelson pitched in. Everyone except Richard, George, and I seemed to be happy with the current sign! The complaint was that the sign was a capital expenditure and the bids brought forward by the Church Council seemed high. In addition to that, the County had ordinances that regulated signs like that, and they should be studied before we take any action. The sign was remanded back to the Church Council for further study."

"The next item on the agenda was the parking lot. Again Richard, George, and Howard Lemke gave a good analysis of the current parking and how adding paved parking would make our church more inviting to visitors. And it might even improve the attendance on rainy days. It was pointed out that this was a capital expenditure also and not a budget item. Again, it was brought up that we were doing very well with the current parking and the question was, do we really need it? It was questioned as to how many visitors we had in any given Sunday."

"The final item was the 'Shepherd of the Sheep Church News Paper'. Howard presented the concept of our congregation going out into the community in a big way. This was backed up by George. I made my case for adopting this approach to the community. I even put for-

ward the idea that we could have this newspaper up and running for Easter. Howard pointed out that this was a budget item in the budget under the Evangelism Budget. The voters voted to table this for further study!"

"Finally, the budget came up for the vote. It was passed with the explicit condition that the Evangelism Board further study the idea of the newspaper and report back at the next quarter Voters Meeting!"

I read this entry. I leaned back in Pastor's chair and the memories of this meeting just swirled around in my head. Pastor hadn't been here a year yet. Usually, when a pastor is new to the congregation, the congregation tries to follow his leadership and go with the suggestions he is making to grow the church. And yet, of all the things he had proposed, the only one that had been accomplished had been the visibility of the church from the road. He had wanted some trees removed and he only got the lower branches removed!

The Annual meeting was historically held in the Fellowship Hall. Usually, it was not that well attended, and seating was no problem. This time, there was an overflow crowd. As I remember, this was a reflection on how effective he was. Because of the crowd, I had suggested that the meeting be moved into the church sanctuary. This would have allowed the accordion doors to be opened to the Fellowship Hall and the overflow seating could be used.

I had made this suggested to a number of Church Council members before the meeting started. Nobody thought that that was a good idea as what went on in the voters' meetings shouldn't take place in the sanctuary in front of the altar. It was my opinion that holding the meeting in the sanctuary would add some discipline to the meeting. I was basically overruled and didn't want to push the point.

Sitting at the table facing the people seated in the Fellowship Hall were the Corporate Secretary Lois Greenback, and Treasurer, Herbert

Gross. Pastor Chuck chose to sit at the back of the room. As I looked out over the members attending, I saw who was seated next to who which allowed me to be able to distinguish the various factions in our church. There was this faction that concentrated on keeping a tight adherence to the biblical interpretation, how it was represented and what was preached. They were very active in the Bible study groups in the church. When a theological issue was raised, they would be the ones debating it. These were some of the older members of the congregation and generally were very strict in their adherence to tradition and that everything was done in *'good order'*.

There was the group that watched over how the money was spent. It was they who made sure that every penny was allocated and accounted for. They were involved with everything down to how much we paid for the communion wine. They were the old guard and very practical in their approach. If it was old and outdated and it broke, fix it; don't replace it with a new updated version. They didn't understand the word progress.

The younger people were more or less scattered around the room. Their interests were centered on the education and activities available to their children. They didn't usually attend the voters' meetings in great numbers but were very supportive of what pastor was doing with the youth. There was also a group of women who were mission minded.

All of these groups were inward focused on strengthening the faith of the congregation members and not on the preaching of the word to the un-churched in the community. What was lacking was outreach.

Things went smoothly with the election. Pastor had a management style that allowed the people on the boards and the volunteers to feel wanted and appreciated. When he met with the boards, he supported their ideas and worked with them to accomplish their plans. His success was reflected in the enthusiasm of the people attending the meeting.

Then the budget came up for adoption. Herbert Gross handed out copies of the budget to all who wished to have a copy. He pointed out that the proposed budget only was about a six and one-quarter increase over the previous one and most of that increase was that Pastor Chuck's salary was higher than was budgeted for in the last budget. That didn't satisfy the old guard! Several of the old guard questioned the increase in the expenditures requested by some of the boards.

Herbert again did his magic and called on the Board Chairmen to explain their increase. This mostly satisfied most of the changes the Chairmen had asked for. Howard Lemke explained outreach through the newspaper. The heated debate that followed was interrupted by one of the younger members making a motion to move the vote on the budget to the end of the meeting. This was immediately seconded by another of the younger members. I was relieved when the person made that motion as I had no idea when it would end.

That took us to Old Business. I have no memory what was discussed. What I remember was that it was getting late, and it was settled very quickly. I remember the younger people were getting restless.

That brought us to New Business. The first item was the Church Council had placed Pastor's request for a new sign on the agenda. Richard gave a history of the sign, that at the time it was put up, this sign design was very popular, and it was state of the art, but times have changed. Pastor Chuck came forward and explained how necessary the new signage was.

His point was that if you drive by you hardly notice it, much less read anything on it. To top it off, since the December Council meeting Richard had obtained three quotes for a sign and then proceeded to present them to the voters. I had encouraged Pastor Chuck to do this as, I thought, it would move things along. In my opinion, the quotes were reasonable. I proposed we do a capital fund drive to pay for the sign, but I wasn't prepared for the pushback.

The arguments against the new sign were that the old sign:
Was a dignified sign that cast our church in a good light.
Was functional as it gave the proper information anyone would want to know.

*And if you wanted to read it, you could drive in the drive-
way to do that.*

And it was in good repair and still looked good.

Some of the younger people spoke in favor of a new sign picking
up Pastor Chucks point that if you didn't know the church was there
you wouldn't even notice it. Finally, someone from the younger group
moved to go forward with the procedure to buy a new sign. It was seconded. The motion was voted down. Another motion was made and
seconded to send the sign proposal back to Church council for further
study. That passed.

The next item under *New Business* was the parking lot. Again,
Richard presented the facts; the paved parking lot was too small. This
time, he came up with some estimates based on the number of parking
spaces to be added. Again, Pastor Chuck reiterated the need for the
church to be looked on as a friendly inviting place.

He pointed out that we had only about thirty-three parking spaces
where the people had access to paving and that parking in the narrow
street was not an option. He pointed out that many of the growing
churches in the area had as many as a hundred parking spaces. That
even the local McDonalds had forty parking spaces. His final question
was what would a visitor to the church think of visiting when he or she
had to park on the grass and walk on the damp grass to get to the paved
part to get to the church door?

If my memory can be trusted the debate that followed went like this:

*There was ample parking area in the grass field behind the
paved parking area.*

We are doing very well with the parking lot as it is.

It had always been adequate in the past.

*The driver could drop people off close to the door and drive
around to park.*

Paving the parking lot was way too expensive.

Some of the younger members were vocal in supporting the parking lot expansion. Their main points were:

The parking on the grass area was a problem especially with small children.

It was messy when it rained.

Several of the women commented that they didn't wear hiking shoes to church.

No matter how early they came for second service, they always had to park on grass.

Finally, one of the younger members moved that we put up signs designating the closest parking spots to the church door as Visitor's parking. Someone seconded the motion. It was questioned as to how many visitors we had on any given Sunday. Someone opposed taking those choice spots and marking them because those spots would probably be empty most of the time! The motion was voted down.

It was pointed out that this was a capital item and that how any expansion of the parking lot would be paid for was the big question. By now, the meeting had been going on for several hours and most of the people who could not see the clock mounted on the wall by the door were looking at their watches. My perception was that many of the people wanted to get this meeting over and soon.

The next item was the '*Shepherd of the Sheep Church News Paper*'. Howard presented the concept to the congregation as the congregation going out into the community. I stepped out of the chair to make a case for this outreach. Pastor Chuck held up a copy of the paper and pointed out how that could be an outreach and it could be possible to have this out in the community by Easter. Howard pointed out that this program fell under the proposed Evangelism Budget. The religious conservatives argued against this as they, the church, would not have input into the general content, the craft, how-to, and other articles, and that could lead to the paper publishing heresy. Again, one of the younger members moved to table this for further study. The motion was seconded and passed.

Finally, the budget was brought up. It was hastily passed with the explicit condition that the Evangelism Board further studies the idea of the newspaper and report back at the next quarter Voters' Meeting. The reason that that meeting was so vivid in my memory was it was the first time Pastor Chuck was really aware of the political factions at work in this church.

PASTOR WALTER'S VISIT

I WAS DREAMING THAT I WAS TIED to a chair and was uncomfortable with my neck in an impossible position when in my dream a phone was ringing. I awoke in Pastor Chuck's desk chair with a crick in my neck to the insistent ringing of Pastor's office phone. I got my senses about me and in my stupor, answered the phone, not so much as to find out who was there but to stop it from ringing. From where I was sitting, I had to turn the chair and reach across the desk for the phone.

"Hello," I answered, probably sounding as if I had been drugged.

"Hello, it's Paul Hessman, I am just checking in with you to see if you have heard anything," he explained. "Did I just wake you?"

"I guess I fell asleep in Pastor's desk chair while I was reading his diary. Right now, it is under his desk," I responded as I tried to find where it had gone. "What have you found out?"

"I called the county sheriff's office and asked what they could do. Their response was that I have to wait 24 hours before I can file a missing person's request. I got the same response from the local police department. I tried to have them just look out for anyone fitting his description, but they have more important things to do," Paul explained.

"Did you contact the local hospitals?" I asked.

"I contacted the hospital with the Emergency Room, but they were no help. Because of the HIPAA law they couldn't give me anything either. So far, I have nothing. I really was calling you to find out if you had discovered anything," Paul said.

"I haven't come up with anything in the diary yet that would explain his absence," I replied.

"It's probably a good idea to keep trying," Paul answered. "I am going to bed and will try the police and the sheriff again in the morning. I should be able to claim it has been 24 hours since anyone had seen him."

"I will look some more into what is written in the diary. Have a good night," I said.

"Goodbye," said Paul.

As the line went dead, I reached forward across the desk and hung up the phone. I rolled Pastor's chair back so I could reach under the desk to retrieve the fallen diary. I inspected it to see if it had suffered any damage when I nodded off and it fell from my hands. I was still trying to be careful with it so as not to leave an indication that I had been reading it.

When I finally was able to get to it, I found that it had fallen open on its face, open to the page with a big green number 36 printed in the upper right-hand corner. Naturally, page 36 of the journal/diary had suffered a very permanent crease diagonally on the page. Well, that damage changed my plan to hide the fact that I had been reading Pastor's diary. No matter how I closed the book you could still see that that page had been damaged.

I checked what was on that page. From what I read and remembered, Pastor Chuck had already been here about a year and one-half. To make sense of what was written I had to turn back to page 35 where I began to read:

"I contacted the District Evangelism about what the Circuit Counselor had told me concerning the training

sessions being held in Detroit, Michigan. This Pastor, Pastor Walter, has been very successful in planting satellite churches and growing them all around the Suburban Detroit area. He is coming through Atlanta to change planes for a week's visit to a mega-church in Orlando. I was wondering if he could stop here to visit our church on his way. Church Council agreed and it is arranged for his visit to take place on Sunday and give us an assessment of things we could do to grow our church."

His next entry read:

"Pastor Walter's visit has been a success. I think he is the answer to my prayers for something to happen to turn this congregation toward outreach into the community. At the Sunday afternoon meeting he pointed out and reinforced many things that needed to be done to grow Shepherd of the Sheep church. He looked at our budget and our giving history. Then between services he walked around our parking lot. From what he saw he suggested we implement a steward ship program. His reasoning was that he could get a feeling about the income of the congregation members by the age and make of cars parked in the lot. He also made a comment about the lack of a modern sign, the lack of visibility, the gravel in the parking lot, the lack of convenient visitor parking, the age and type of the décor in our women's bathroom and a number of other minor things. He drove home the idea that a growing church has to be very inviting to visitors and keep up with the times. As a result of his visit, we are sending four members to his church training session in a month. This is very exciting."

Reading these two entries made me look for what he had written once the four men came back from the Detroit training sessions. I looked further and found what Pastor Chuck wrote later.

> *"The four men sent up to the training in Detroit really had their eyes opened to what church growth really looks like. I am enthused about the materials they came back with. We might finally have a workable program to use within the community!"*

I leaned back in Pastor's chair and wished I had the courage to put my feet up on Pastor's desk and get really comfortable, but out of respect that never happened. The memories of that visit four and on-half years ago, though, were unforgettable. After Rev. Walter was safely on his way to the airport, Pastor Chuck and I drove separately to the local Denny's for a long cup of coffee. It being Sunday evening, the restaurant was virtually empty and we were confident that no one from church would interrupt or overhear us. We got a table and Pastor ordered black coffee with a sweet roll and I ordered the same.

"George, Pastor Walter's assessment was just what the congregation needed to hear! I have been trying to make these points since I came, but most of it has passed by their ears!"

"Well, we trimmed back the trees and graveled over the grass parking area, that was some progress," I defensively pointed out.

Pastor Chuck continued, "he pointed out something that I have been praying about for some time, the faith and giving state of the congregation. He talked privately to me about the giving history in our church when he looked over our books. As far as demographics go, our giving is on the low side for congregations our size. One of the ways he judged that was based on the cars in our parking lot. He made that statement in when he was talking to the congregation."

"Yah, that part kind 'a shocked the congregation. From where I sat at the front facing the people, I could see the look on their faces. They really didn't take that very well," was my come back.

"Then he mentioned the sign. Now, that it is recognized that our sign is antiquated, how long do we have to argue about the size and the wording on it before we act to get it replaced?" he questioned.

"I don't have an answer," I replied.

"He even suggested that at least half of the pine trees in front of the church be cut down to make the church more visible! How long have I been pushing for that? Maybe he got that point across!" he hopefully stated.

"I don't know about that one, it seemed to go over their heads." I replied.

"I know George that you worked hard to get the gravel for the grass parking lot, but he really made the point that it should be asphalt. He also pointed out that we still should make that lot bigger. It was good that they heard it from someone from outside the congregation, an expert." Pastor continued as he looked at a slip of paper he had pulled from his pocket.

Our waitress came up behind me holding a coffee pot.

"Can I refresh your coffee?" she asked.

"Mine's okay," I answered.

Pastor held his up and she filled it.

I continued, "Pastor Walter really hit on a lot of good points. Even things you haven't brought up yet. I thought his mentioning the visitor's parking and other things like the women's bathroom also made the members aware of how much needs to be done around here to make this place more inviting."

Pastor Chuck pointed out, "When you asked Pastor Walter if there would be room at his next training session to send some of our members to it, I was surprised. Then when Howard Lemke suggested that from the money in his budget the congregation could send four people, I couldn't believe it."

"When Pastor Walter said there would be room for four more people, I made the commitment that we would send them. Church Council has the authority to do that, and I believe I can get it through," I answered, going out on a limb, but making the commitment.

We talked some more and drank our coffee. I paid the bill, left a sizable tip, and we left. Pastor seemed happy with the results of that meeting.

Howard Lemke took the lead in getting Council to approve the funds for the training session in Detroit. The problem came down to who to send. Howard had been trying all sorts of things to promote church growth, most only small programs with no discernible results. He was looking for ideas that could be used in our community.

The program with the biggest potential of bringing our church into the community had been the News Paper. That was opposed by the old guard as a waste of money and the 'Purists' on theological grounds. Although Pastor would have a half page to use for the furtherance of God's word and we would have church activities advertised throughout the paper, the Theological Purists objected to the lack of control of the other articles. We continued to debate it, but it became a moot point when a neighboring church picked up the program. Howard never got over that. Pastor went on to pray about other things.

We were slowly growing with northerners who were being moved into the area by companies such as Ford Motor Company and GM, but these were not originally from the local community. As I remember it, back then the Board of Evangelism was composed of Howard and four more members elected by the congregation. Howard had a new member Joe Turley who had been elected to his board at the last Annual Meeting. He was one of the members transferred to the area by GM from one of its northern plants. He was very enthusiastic about spreading the gospel in our community and was very supportive of any ideas Pastor and Howard had, so he was chosen as one to attend.

Howard would lead the group. Glen Rich, the head Elder, was chosen to go as the Elders would become a part of any spiritual growth of the new members. Jeff Gage, head of the Board of Stewardship, would go as new member giving was always something to be considered. The Council felt that whatever these men could learn in these areas would be very important.

As I was going through these old memories from five and a half years ago, a new memory came to mind. When you drink a lot of coffee as I had done all night, at some point it would want to come out. I decided to get out of the chair and take a walk to take care of that memory.

THE RESULTS FROM
THE DETROIT TRIP

THE WALK I TOOK AROUND IN THE church led me by the secretary's office. I was feeling a little thirsty and thought about getting a drink of water from the bubbler, but then I checked and there was still a little coffee left from our earlier meetings and I decided even cold coffee would taste better than ambient temperature water. With a new cup of coffee in hand, I sat back down in Pastor's chair and picked up his diary again.

If my memory serves me right, Howard and the group he headed returned from the training session just before the start of Lent. With all the activity taking place at Shepherd of the Sheep Church that spring, Pastor Chuck was very busy during Lent.

George Michaelson had been very successful working with the youth group and since Pastor Chuck had come, the youth group had grown. That year's confirmation class was the largest in the history of our congregation and required a lot of Pastor's times preparing the confirmands for confirmation on Palm Sunday. He chose to meet with each confirmand and his or her parents.

Pastor Chuck had decided Lenten Service sermons for this year would be of a historical nature centered on the disciples. That meant he had to prepare eight sermons for the weeknight services. Then there were the six Sunday's that needed sermons. And finally, the Easter Sunday service needed a strong sermon.

Howard, Glenn, and Jeff reported to Church Council at the next meeting, but it was not until after Easter that the group that had gone to Detroit met with Pastor Chuck. I think each one had talked to Pastor about the training, but with what was going on, Pastor didn't schedule a meeting until a couple of weeks after Easter.

He talked to me about the delay in meeting with the group that had attended the Detroit training. His plan was to meet with them about two weeks after Easter when the Board of Evangelism regularly meets. With all of the sermons he had to prepare and the meetings with each of the confirmands with their families, he just didn't have the time to do it before Easter! I agreed with him, he needed time after Easter to catch up with the activities of the other boards after he had been so focused on Lent, confirmation, and Easter.

Glenn and the rest of the Elders backed him up on that decision. Howard understood that it would take several long meetings with Pastor to cover what they had learned, and it would take time to analyze the data and how to effectively apply it to Shepherd of the Sheep Church. He wanted the whole board to be involved.

Jeff Gage had been applying what he had learned and was already laying the plans for the fall Stewardship drive. He felt that pastor would be pleased with what things he could show him. He was excited by what he saw.

It was the new member, Joe Turley, elected to Howard's Evangelism Board where the trouble began. Joe was so impressed by what he saw at the church in Detroit that he wanted to hit the ground running with new ideas on how to restructure our church. I remember clearly how he approached me about the third week of Lent with the revisions he wanted to make to the constitution to enable such changes.

I immediately asked him if he had mentioned any of this to Pastor. His answer was that Pastor had put him off until after Easter! This upset him. And anyway, this was, in his way of thinking, a Church Council concern and not a concern of the pastor. Wasn't the pastor an employee of the congregation and therefore didn't have any say on how the church was run?

I had to explain to Joe that in our denomination the pastorate was a called position that the call is for life, that we as a congregation, call a pastor to lead us. The corporate structure is put in place to cover the physical details of operating the facility and complying with the laws of the state in regard to property, how we pay our staff, and what we believe as Christians. The purpose of this was to allow the pastor to tend to the spiritual needs of the congregation without being bogged down with the physical details of running the church.

Therefore, whenever we, as a congregation, contemplate changing our corporate structure, we involve the pastor in that decision. And then if there are any changes to the constitution, they have to be presented to the district for approval. If he wishes to do something, he should first discuss it with the board chairman, which was Howard in this case. Then take it to the board and the pastor.

This didn't sit well with him. He had already talked to some of his friends and shared his ideas with them. And he was upset that Pastor hadn't sat down immediately and listened. I alerted Howard about the situation. Howard met with Joe personally and met with the people Joe had talked with. In the end, they agreed that Lent, confirmation, and Easter Sunday took priority over assessing right away what had been learned.

I looked through the pages of the diary and Pastor hadn't made any reference to this situation, so I don't think he even knew about it. He made a number of entries about how exhilarating and exhausting this Lenten season had become, but the joy of what the Lord was doing was the answer to his prayers.

It was two weeks after Easter when Howard presided over the first board meeting that included the group that had gone to Detroit. The week before the meeting, Howard had given Pastor and me a Xerox copy of the materials that were covered during the training. They were broken down into several sections.

Section 1 covered what to do to make your 'Campus' more inviting to outsiders visiting your campus for the first time.

Section 2 covered how visitors should be treated to make them feel welcomed but not overwhelmed when they visited for the first time.

Section 3 covered how best to follow up with the visitors once they showed interest in the church.

Section 4 covered integrating the new members into congregational life.

Section 5 covered starting satellite churches.

I thought Pastor was impressed with the material Howard and his group had brought back. Then I read what he had written in his Diary.

> "Howard gave me a copy of the materials covered at the Evangelism Training session in Detroit. It seems to be a thorough assessment as to what needs to be done to grow a church once the visitors come in the door. The question not answered was how to get the people onto the campus and through the door in the first place. What was the hook or program that they used? From what I could determine, it was the campus that attracted the people. The people we sent have indicated that they were very impressed with what has been taking place at that congregation. Did they ask the right questions when they were there?"

> "I am meeting with them the second week after Easter and plan to go over what they have learned. Maybe

the materials didn't cover what was presented in the meetings. Maybe they learned what it is that attracts the visitors to the campus in the first place from what was discussed in the meetings. I have prayed for an answer to this for so long. I hope I find that answer here. I have great hope for this meeting."

Pastor's next entry pertaining to the training in Detroit was as follows:

"I met for over 2 hours with the Howard, the board and the group that attended the training session. George Harrelson also attended the meeting. Howard was very pleased to show off what the team had learned. I think he was trying to justify the expense of attending the training. He had all of the people who attended the training give a report. I think Jeff was the most enthusiastic about having been there. I never realized how unprepared he had felt he had been to run a Stewardship Drive. I should have been more helpful in the one last fall. I looked at his plan then, but I was more involved with "making Shepherd of the Sheep Church" a more inviting place. Glen Rich's report on how the Elders were impacted by church growth was what we already were doing. The only thing he came away with was to give the new members more mentoring. We had never assigned a church family to mentor a new family and that sounded like a positive thing to do. Joe, the new member of the Evangelism Board who attended was very impressed with the idea of starting satellite churches and spent some time explaining the process. Of the group, no one had any insight as to how to get visitors onto the campus. The board plans to meet again in two weeks and at that time, I plan

*to probe the memories of the people to see if I can uncover
any answer to how they 'Grow the Church'."*

I remember attending that first meeting with Howard's board. To start it off, he asked for someone to tell what he had learned from the training sessions. The first one to pipe up was Jeff, Chairman of the Stewardship Board. He explained that the person leading the class spent a lot of time describing how their church was set up to welcome the prospective members into the congregation and gently lead them through the idea that membership involved Time, Talent, and Treasure.

The sessions pertaining to integrating the prospect into the life of the congregation were for him the most interesting. What was also the most helpful to him was the list of organizations that provide printed material that is available for use during the Fall Stewardship drive. He was already using this information to work with Pastor for this year's drive. He also mentioned talking with others that attended the session about what they were handling Stewardship in their congregations. He stated that those discussions after class were almost as enlightening as those that took place in class.

During Jeff's report, I remember Pastor asking some rather pointed questions, but for the life of me I can't remember what they were anymore. I remember some of Glenn's report and the fact that Pastor and Glen were planning to bring a program to the Church Council to mentor the new members. By the time Joe brought up the satellite church idea, I remember it took a long time and I was too tired to remember any details. What I remember taking away from that meeting was that we seemed to be making progress.

ACCOLADES AND REBELLION

I CONTINUED LOOKING THROUGH THE PAGES OF the diary until I found a reference to the next meeting with Howard's Board. From the headings I saw on the pages I skipped through, I noticed what Pastor was doing with the other boards. He was encouraging them to think of ways to venture into the community. From the comments I saw, he was not having much success. He did write a short paragraph in reference to the spring quarterly Voters Assembly Meeting.

His comments,

> *"the Voters Assembly Meeting accomplished nothing. Howard's report on the trip to Detroit was that the results will be presented during the June meeting. Nothing was done with the Old Business to move the items forward and no New Business was brought forward. All I can do is pray!"*

During that time, he and I were meeting regularly before the Church Council meetings, but my workload at the Insurance office had become heavier as my business was expanding. The number of companies we were representing was growing which required more of my time. At church I was focused on Church Growth so I, as church President, was concentrating on the Board of Evangelism and wasn't much help with what he was doing with the other boards.

I made it a point to attend the *specially* called Evangelism Board meeting. Howard called the meeting to order. I remember it lasted for over two hours. The discussion centered around what that church in Detroit offered to bring people onto the campus and how that worked. I don't remember any conclusions, so reading what pastor wrote was very interesting.

> *"I met with Howard's board to see what they had learned from the discussions during the classes on the subjects that were taught. What I really wanted to know was how that church attracted the new members that were contributing to the church growth that they were experiencing. We had a long discussion on how the campus, that was what they called their church grounds, might appear to a stranger. From what our people described, they had transformed the property into what a small college campus looks like. The building complex is set up in such a way as not to look threatening. Although their visit was in the winter, there were only a couple of inches of snow on the ground and they were impressed by the 'Park-like' appearance of the campus. It looked friendly and inviting were the words they used to describe it. If you were a non-Christian, you can feel comfortable coming to any meeting on their campus. That is their intent."*
>
> *"Once inside the buildings, the décor is that of respecting the age of the architecture, but with the look of a modern building. The walls look pristine, and the floors appeared polished, but not slippery. Howard was impressed at how clean and shiny the floors were with all of the snow and dirt that was continually tracked in from the outside.*

Again, the inside is modern looking and up to date. There are signs posted on the walls inside the corridors pointing to various classrooms, offices, bathrooms, and other points of interest a person might want to find. The complex is old, but easy for a person to find their way around. In some respects, I should have insisted that Richard Nelson, head Trustee, had gone. Maybe he would have gone wild putting up signs in all of our hallways."

"The rooms where the meetings were held were also a revelation. Glen Rich was impressed by the amount of time that was spent in the meetings. He has difficulty sitting on the metal folding chairs we have in our meeting rooms. His comments about the meeting rooms centered around what is in the meeting rooms. The chairs were not the metal folding chairs we have in all our rooms; no, they are the comfortable padded stackable chairs. And he was actually comfortable sitting through the three-hour meetings they had! The chairs are set up with folding tables so the people attending the presentations have a writing surface on which to take notes. The rooms, there are two of them, are each set up with a slide projector and a video tape player projector. This makes it easy for the presenter to communicate with those attending. There is also a white board on the wall for the presenter to use. Howard described a facility that impressed him, but he didn't mention any way to fill it."

"I told them to talk to each other to see if they could remember the discussions they attended that indicated how that congregation attracted new members. Note to myself! At the next scheduled Evangelism Board meeting I will make sure that we have a report for the next Council meeting."

I paged ahead until I found the entry for the next meeting; I attended that meeting.

"This is the third meeting of Howard's board to address the Detroit training sessions. We came up with a number of things that might bring people onto our 'Campus'. The first thing that was mentioned was to make our campus more 'Park-like', to make it more inviting. The list of suggestions were:

Redo the shrubbery around the church.

Finally take some action on modernizing our church sign.

Extend and pave the parking lot.

Have designated visitor's parking spots.

Have the women of the church get together to upgrade the décor in our church to make it more friendly.

Increase our advertising budget to promote religious observances and holidays.

Have outdoor banners to announce upcoming events.

Make it known that our campus is available to other groups to use for some secular activities.

Find a need in the community and fill it.

See what activities we can sponsor for the use of our forested area that is essentially not used, after all we have four acres back there.

That is the list that Howard agreed to bring to the next council meeting."

I attended that board meeting and was impressed by how Pastor handled that meeting. He asked Howard to give him time to start a discussion and out of that discussion came those suggestions. Joe, the other board member that attended the training sessions with Howard, was adamant in his contention that what was proposed was all wrong and superficial. The way to grow the church was to start satellite churches around the area.

He was unyielding and had argued a long time for that point. Pastor countered that we needed to first grow where we were before we could branch out. The report Howard made at the May Church Council Meeting was essentially what Pastor had written in his diary.

The May Church Council meeting, I remember, lasted a long time. Again, it is fuzzy in my memory, and I have to think on this, but the only item that was impressed on my mind was Howard's Board of Evangelism report. As I remember it, and I may be wrong, Howard led off his report with the statement that the way to encourage church growth was to get our message out into the community.

"To do this we must be seen and what is seen affects how our message will be received. How our message will be received by non-Christian members of our community will be how we appear to them. Are we a dowdy looking place that is just there, or are we an inviting place that people will feel uplifted when they are on our campus? The growing church we visited in Detroit has a very uplifting campus where people can come and participate in many activities."

He then described the campus, the meeting rooms, and the *park-like* atmosphere. He then suggested that in order to bring our campus up to the standards of the one they visited in Detroit, we would need to do many things. Howard then read off the list of things that came from the Detroit training sessions. As he read off the list, the council members began shaking their heads and looking like '*is this for real?*' Then the discussion began. Where will we get the money for the parking lot, do you realize how much that will cost? Maybe we could do the cheap things first.

Then Pastor Chuck stood up to speak. He picked up the list of things that the Evangelism Board had come up with and read through each of them. As he read each one, he asked if that one had merit. No one on Church Council could dispute any of the items on the list. Then he reminded them of what they had called him to do as a pastor. He asked them rhetorically if he has been successful as their spiritual leader to grow them in the faith. He asked them rhetorically if he had been successful in bringing The Word of God into the community. He then asked them to vote to bring Howard's report to the June Congregation Voters Assembly.

After the motion passed, Billy Jackson, Board of Finance; Jeff Gage, Board of Stewardship; and Herbert Gross, Treasurer, discussed how to raise the money. The Council then voted to present special capital improvements drive to cover the cost of the improvements to the Voters Assembly. I remember I was sure glad when that meeting was over.

I turned the page in his diary and found his description on that May Council meeting. Pastor had written,

"*The Council meeting went long, but my prayers have been answered! Ann Helgeson presented her Vacation Bible School extra budget item which was approved. Emily Windsor reported on the Social Ministry June Ice Cream Social Event. It took some doing, but Howard's list of improvements for church growth were approved to be an Old Business agenda item for the June Voters Assembly meeting. Also, in New Business, will be a capital funding drive. Finally, we will begin getting into the community!*"

One entry that caught my eye was a doodle. It appeared to be a face looking reverently at hands folded in prayer. Beneath it Pastor had written,

"*I am in awe of what happened this Sunday! First service was very light, and I had wondered what I had done wrong for this to happen. None of the regulars were there. At 10:25, I stepped into the sacristy to begin the second service and saw that the Second service was standing room only full, so they had opened the wall and the congregation spilled into the Fellowship Hall. I didn't know what to think. What had caused this? Am I so far out of the loop that I missed something? Was it something I had done? I pondered this all through the service. At the end of the service, George came up the center aisle and began to address me. I didn't know what to expect. He announced to me and the congregation that this was the second anniversary of my installation and the congregation wanted to do something to celebrate it. He handed me an envelope and instructed me to take my family out to a restaurant for dinner. This was a total surprise and a great relief. I am so thankful!"*

My memory of that Sunday was one of surprise. Glen Rich and the Elders had felt that Pastor had been doing a great job. So, they decided to honor him by recognizing the anniversary of his second year. They all contacted their people and planned this surprise. I couldn't believe so many people kept that secret! I only found out about it before the service when Glen handed me the envelope and told me what to say when I presented it. I guess I was as out of touch with what was happening as Pastor!

I skipped a number of short entries dealing with the other boards that were preparing for the Voters Assembly. The next long entry Pastor made was after the June Voters Assembly.

"Tonight, was the longest Voters Assembly yet. At 7:00 p. m., George gaveled the meeting to order. I had great hope for what could be accomplished in bringing Shepherd of the Sheep Church into the community. I had worked with all of the boards so their reports should project the forward movement of the church. Ann Helgeson's report on the strides she has taken to take the Vacation Bible School to new heights by opening it up to the community was well received. Emily Windsor's report on the coming Ice Cream Social and how it would be advertised in the community got a round of applause. Richard Nelson's report on the improvements he made to the sink in the women's bathroom was received by some woman commenting 'finally' from the

floor. Then Howard got up and reported that the Evangelism Board had had several meetings and the details from those meetings would be covered under Old Business. It was already pretty late when we got around to that. Howard read the report that the Council had voted on. The report was not well received. It was debated. Joe, the member of Howard's board and had attended the Detroit training sessions, stood up and attacked Howard and me as doing the wrong thing and not planting satellite churches. George thanked him for his opinion and the debate continued. The old sign controversy was brought up. Action on Council's recommendation on Howard's report was tabled for further study. Then, New Business was brought to the floor. At that time, the financing of the whole project was addressed. The whole thing was tabled for more study. How can things go from the celebration of my second year here to this resistance to everything I have prayed about? Won't they ever learn that "Go ye therefore" doesn't mean back to your seat and sit? I must keep praying."

I looked at the next entry and it appeared he skipped a month or two. I remember that meeting well. I decided to hold that meeting in the church sanctuary with the wall to the Fellowship Hall closed. Seating was tight, but I wanted it there. I expected that Howard's report and the action that the Council had taken would result in some heated discussions. *I was right.*

I think meeting in the church in front of the unlit altar had a calming effect on the debate that came up during the Business part of the meeting. It was agreed that all of the points brought up in the report were valid. The question was, were they necessary for the church to grow? The argument was we serving the new people who were being transferred into our area, and weren't we growing?

Pastor made the point that we were not a part of the community and that was what he was called to change. What was very upsetting was the grandstanding made by the member of Howard's board about the satellite churches. That felt like a stab in the back for the Council and to Pastor's leadership!

The afternoon after the meeting I met Pastor at the Denny's for coffee and a roll. I wanted our meeting to be private with no church interruptions. Our church usually had volunteers wandering around doing things on many days. In here we could talk without being seen or overheard. I arrived first and had the waitress seat me at a table that was out of the way and in a corner. I caught his attention when he arrived and waved him over.

As he was approaching the table I spoke, "you don't look that battered!"

"You don't know how I feel," he responded.

"Maybe I do, at least a little The Council took a beating last night too," I answered.

"What hurt the worst was the implication that I don't know what I'm doing by Joe Turley, the member of Howard's board, the very member I thought was on my side!" he gloomily explained.

"That one hit me pretty hard too," I responded.

"What am I doing wrong? Is it my sermons? Why am I not getting through to them?" he questioned. "I've prayed and prayed over this and every answer that I seem to have, have been rejected."

"I don't know about that. Emily seemed to get support for her Ice Cream Social and it might bring a few curious members of the community and the Vacation Bible School should bring in some of the children from around the church. She did say she would post the invitation in the local stores, didn't she?" I observed.

"Advertising that was not her original idea. Her original one was a nostalgic get together for the congregation. Bringing in outsiders never occurred to her!" he corrected me.

"Well then, you are getting results," I suggested.

"Last summer, we did have a Vacation Bible School, but it was not well attended. At least this year we have advertised by having the youth walk around the neighborhood and place invitations on the door of every home. Ann has done a great job putting the program together, but after last night, I wonder," he mused.

"I feel sort of responsible for last night," I commented. "I should have worked closer with you and Howard to spread what the Council had approved. You know, we should get together more often and just dream."

"What do you mean, just dream?" he asked.

"Just sit and kick around ideas. Maybe ideas you have and are praying about. Maybe we could work together and come up with a strategy. For instance, no one has forbidden us from making a banner advertising Emily's Ice Cream Social for the neighborhood to see." I suggested.

"Yeah, that might be helpful," he replied.

"Have you thought of a restaurant to take your family to yet?" I asked trying to steer the conversation in a happier direction.

"Not yet. We think we will find a good one downtown though," he replied.

"May I suggest PittyPat's Porch in downtown Atlanta. It emotes the nostalgia of the Old South and would be an interesting experience for the kids too," I suggested.

"That gift took me by surprise. I didn't know what to think. I had no clue!" he stated.

"They took me by surprise, too. The first I knew about it was when Glen handed me the envelope and the script about five minutes before Second Service," I replied.

We talked for a time about family things. Our meeting ended on a happier note.

I looked at the clock and saw 1:24 and decided I needed sleep, so I went and sprawled out on the pleather couch.

A PLACE TO BEGIN LOOKING

THIS MORNING, I WOKE UP ON THE couch in Pastor's office when the morning sun came streaming through the window. It looks to be a bright and cloudless June day, the kind of a day when you would like to play hooky from work and go fishing or something. Unfortunately, I immediately became aware of my surroundings and remembered why I had spent the night here. I immediately headed for the restroom. After doing the necessary things and splashing some water on my face to make sure I was awake, I headed back to Pastor's office.

I called Paul Hessman at 6:45 a. m. to check in with him before he headed to work.

The phone rang.

"Hello, you have reached the Hessman's," Paul answered.

"Hello Paul, it's Gorge, just checking in with you before you head for work," I told him.

"I have had a quiet night, not that I slept well, but no one called or anything. I called work and am taking a personal day to help in any way I can," he replied.

"Nothing happened here other than I read more in his diary," I replied. "I did get some sleep though."

"I plan to call the police and the sheriff's departments when I get off the phone with you to get the missing person paperwork started. Then I'll come over to church so you can go home. We can make a plan when I get there," he stated.

"That sounds good to me. See ya soon," I replied and hung up.

At 8:00 a.m., I called in to my office to tell them to cancel and reschedule all appointments for today and tomorrow. I gave them instructions to call me at home if an emergency should occur and at the church number if they couldn't reach me at home. Paul arrived while I was still on the phone with my office, came in, saluted me, and seated himself in the upholstered chair. I looked over at him sitting. He appeared tired, with lines on his face that I didn't remember seeing before.

"You made good time," I said as I hung up the phone.

"You don't look well rested. Did you have a bad night?" he asked.

"Believe it or not I don't feel that bad. It must be the leftover coffee from the Elders meeting last night," I replied.

"I assume you have this morning's pot brewed already," he stated.

"I didn't get around to that yet, I was waiting for you to take care of that. I have been thinking of what has to be done and then I was on the phone to my office. I wanted to check with you, though, before I called Helen," I answered.

"What are you going to tell her?" Paul asked.

"I guess that we don't know anything yet, but we are here at church making phone calls. You have anything you would add?" I responded.

"No, that just about covers it," he responded.

I picked up the phone and dialed the number for the parsonage. The phone rang about five times before it was answered.

"Hello Berg residence, Liz Harrelson speaking. Can I take a message?" was the response.

"It's me, George," was my reply.

"Oh George, it's so good you called. We are worried sick over here. Helen didn't get much sleep; the kids are full of questions and things are hectic right now. We sent the kids off to the special summer program at school thinking that keeping them occupied would be good for them. Helen is beside herself with worry and don't know what to do with herself," Liz reported.

As I listened, I was trying to think of something to say. All I could do was listen.

Helen continued, "what have you found out? What are you doing? We need answers!"

"Here is what I know, Paul called around last night and found nothing. He will call the sheriff's office and the police department and file a missing person's report this morning. He has to wait 24 hours to do that. Calling the hospitals doesn't do any good because of the HIPAA rules. Paul has taken a personal day off work and will be available to do whatever needs to be done. I've called the office and told my crew that I will be out of the office for two days. I plan to go home and freshen up and be back here at church at least by 10:00. I haven't eaten breakfast yet, but in all this excitement I am not even hungry," I told her.

"Well, the kids will be at school until noon and available if we need to contact any of them. That leaves Helen and me here in this empty house to wonder. Why don't Helen and I come to the church and do what we can. Maybe we can help with the phones. At least that will keep Helen occupied and, in the loop," Liz suggested.

"That sounds like a good plan. I have to hang up, Helga Bakemeir, the office secretary, just walked in," I explained as I hung up the phone.

"Hi, where is Pastor?" asked Helga, as she walked through the door.

"He isn't here," I responded.

"Well, yesterday he promised to have the Sunday's bulletin ready for me to cut the stencil and run off the bulletins on the Gestetner," she replied.

"So, you saw him yesterday morning?" asked Paul.

"Yeah, Jack Ernst was with him. They were going to breakfast at the I-HOP, I think," she replied.

"Did they say when they would be back?" I asked.

"No, but I didn't expect them back before I usually leave or he would've asked me to wait for the bulletin," she replied.

"There was a pretty tough Voters Assembly meeting Monday night and he stayed over. What kind of a mood was he in when you saw him?" Paul questioned.

"Well," she thought for a minute before answering, "he didn't seem happy. To think of it, Jack wasn't his usual self either. I think they had been talking about something. I think Pastor Chuck said something about fresh air. It was a nice sunny day when I drove in."

"How long are you going to stay around this morning seeing as you don't have the bulletin information yet?" I asked.

"I suppose I'll go home. Other than the bulletin, there is really nothing I do around here unless Pastor Chuck has some letters he wants typed."

"Pastor is missing," Paul told her. "You were probably the last one to see him yesterday."

"Oh my!" Helga exclaimed as her face turned ashen and she, an older lady in her 60's, grabbed on to the door frame to keep her balance.

"That is why anything more you can tell us this morning might be helpful for us to find him," Paul explained.

Helga took a moment to catch her breath and answered, "Jack had his Jeep parked by the back door and I think they left together in that as Pastor's car was still in the lot when I got here. That jeep of his! What is an 82-year-old widower running around in something as dangerous as that? It doesn't even have doors!" she exclaimed.

Paul jumped into action, "I'll go down to Helga's office and start working the phone. First, I'll see if I can get in touch with Jack. If he's not home, I'll try his son and see if he knows where he would be. If I can't find anything out doing that, then I'll contact the sheriff's department and the police department with this information and add that to the missing person's report, I made earlier. Then I'll head over to the I-HOP and see if anyone remembers seeing Pastor and Jack there yesterday."

With that Paul headed for Helga's office.

"Helga, Liz and Helen are on their way to the church to help. They can cover the phones. The church is the central coordination point where everyone involved has been told to call. We will use Pastor's office as the base as that is where the comfortable furniture is. I will clear a large spot-on Pastor's desk to make a place for you to write and take notes. Can you stay around and answer the phones until they get here? I need to go home, eat breakfast, and clean up. I should be back at least by at least 10:30 if not sooner. Is that okay?" I asked her as I began to systematically pile some of the papers on his desk.

"I'll do that; I might even stay around and be what help I can," she responded.

"Good, I'm leaving, good luck," I said as I headed for the door.

When I got back a little after 10:00, I was welcomed by Liz, Helen, and Paul. Helga had left when Paul got back.

"Oh, good your back. Paul just got back from the I-HOP. Helen and I were holding down the fort. Bill Stricker called wanting to know if you had found anything yet. He said the phone was so busy that this was the first time he could get through. Henry Paulsen and Glen Rich called, and each offered to go out and search. Howard Lemke called and asked if he could do something. Fred Ernst's wife called and gave me his work number so you can call him there," Liz reported.

Helen was sitting on the couch and said, "hi", as I came in.

"How are you?" I asked her as I went over to where she was sitting.

"Worried and scared," she replied. "Liz has helped me a lot."

I was about to respond when Paul spoke, "I called the police department and gave them what we know. I have to go down there and sign some papers, but they have begun looking for the Jeep. I did the same with the sheriff's department and will have to go there also. I tried to call Fred at his home, he's Jack's son and an Engineer at Scientific Atlanta. I left a message on his answering machine.

"I went to the I-HOP and spoke to the manager. He knows Jack as he is a regular and usually eats alone, so when business is slow the manager generally comes over and talks to him. The manager said he was surprised when Jack came in with another person for breakfast. He was so surprised that he came over and was introduced to Pastor Chuck by Jack. They even commented that it looked to be good day for going for a ride. He didn't know where they were going, though." Paul concluded.

"Here is Fred's work number," Liz said as she handed Paul a note.

"I'm heading over to the church office to call him now. Maybe I can reach him before his lunch break," said Paul as he left.

"Did you get much sleep last night?" Liz asked as I positioned one of the visitor's chairs in a way that I could see Liz across the desk from where Helen was sitting on the couch.

"I think I might have gotten about four hours." was my answer.

"I don't think Helen and I got a lot more. Neither of us could sleep so we just sat and talked," Liz answered.

"Did Helga fill you in on what we had found out from her?" I asked.

"She said something about Jack Ernst being here and them leaving together in his Jeep, but there was not time for much else. We had just got here and then Paul arrived from the I-HOP and she left," Liz replied.

"Did Paul get a chance to fill you in on what we know?" I asked.

"No, he was about to when you got back," she answered.

"Well, from what we heard we think that Jack got here early and was talking to Pastor Chuck when Helga got here to pick up the bulletin to prepare it for Sunday. He didn't have it ready. He and Jack then left to go to I-HOP, and you heard the rest from Paul. As far as we know, the two of them are together somewhere without a phone or they would have contacted someone," I postulated.

"So, you think he's alright?" Helen tearfully stated.

"At this time, I think no news is good news," I responded.

Helen had been sitting quietly on the couch during this whole discussion. I was beginning to wonder what was going through her mind. The time was approaching, 11:00 and I was wondering why Paul hadn't come back yet.

"Liz, do you need to go home and check on things?" I asked.

"No, Helen and I will stop for a moment, and I will pick up a few things on our way to the parsonage. We came in my car, and we should leave soon as the kids will be home from the school summer program a little after 12:00," Helen stated.

Paul came hurriedly through the door and announced, "I just got off the phone with Fred. I called him, and his office has several lines so while I was on the line with him, he was able to phone several neighbors. None of them saw the Jeep in the carport at the house last night and it isn't there now. No one saw him at the house last night either. It's good weather and he usually is out in the yard when the weather is good. He has a cabin in the mountains near Dahlonega. When the weather is good, he likes to take the Jeep and drive up there for the day. Fred thinks that is probably what he has done. He probably stopped by and invited Pastor to go with him. If that is the case, Pastor is probably with him. It's not like him to spend the night up there, especially since Pastor is with him, so something must have happened. Fred is taking the afternoon off from work and I am meeting him at his house as soon as I can get there. We are going to drive up to the cabin and see what we can find," Paul hurriedly explained.

"That news is encouraging, at least we have a place to begin looking," I responded.

"That gives me hope," Helen tearfully responded.

"I'll call and check in here at the church when we find anything," Paul reassured us as he was preparing to leave.

"Let's pray," I said as I bowed my head and folded my hands and began to pray.

At the end of my prayer all said "Amen". And Paul went out the door.

"Helen and I need to leave too as the kids will be at the parsonage in less than an hour," Liz said, and they both got up ready to leave the office.

"I'm going to go to McDonald's drive thru and pick up a Big Mac for lunch and come right back to cover the phone. It should only take me about fifteen minutes. If anyone calls, the answering machine will take a message and I can answer it when I get back," I told them.

We left and I locked the church door.

THE SEARCH BEGINS

It was a little before noon when I returned with my lunch bag and a Coke from McDonald's. I decided to eat it in the boardroom as that wouldn't create crumbs in Pastor's office, it was near the bathroom, and it was close to the phone in the church secretary's office. Needless to say, the phone was silent, and I ate in peace.

Things had quieted down and my adrenaline surge had finally worn off. The way I felt it seemed like my lack of sleep had had finally caught up with me. I sat there on an uncomfortable folding chair at a folding table; staring at an empty McDonald's bag lying next to an open, empty McDonald's Big Mac box; holding in my hand an empty paper cup of Coke, the straw from which I had just gurgled the last bit of liquid. I felt exhausted!

I finally pulled myself together and made my way back to the 'control center' which was the Pastor's office, to a comfortable chair to await any phone calls that might come in. As I sat in that comfortable chair, I looked over at the more comfortable looking couch and decided it looked lonely and unloved, therefore being the loving fellow that I am, I decided to go over and do the right thing and lay down on it.

It was about 2:00 when the phone rang, startling me during my nap. It took me a while to get up to the desk to answer it.

"Hello, can I help you?" I answered in a groggy voice as I stood by the desk and answered it.

"Did I wake you up?" Liz asked.

"Yeah," I answered with a yawn.

"Just checken in with you to see if you had heard anything yet; things are pretty 'worried' here at the parsonage and we were just wondering," Liz responded.

I could hear Helen in the background shushing the younger kids who were seemingly very upset over their dad being missing. I could only imagine the fear and anxiety felt by Helen and the kids.

"Nothing yet, I don't think Paul and Fred have had enough time to reach the cabin. I don't think there is phone service at the cabin anyway," I answered.

I actually had no idea if this was true, but Jack is a frugal man, and I couldn't see him paying for phone service to a cabin he rarely visits. I said that to buy more time in their minds for Paul and Fred to search for them.

"Let us know if you find out anything." Liz pleaded.

"I will, goodbye," I said.

"Goodbye," Liz said, and the phone went click.

I hung up the phone and sat down in Pastor's chair. I hadn't gotten a long enough nap and the taste in my mouth was that of cotton, I was still a little groggy but looking at the clock, I could see that Paul and Fred should reach the cabin soon and if I would fall asleep again, I would only feel worse. My thinking was to re-pile the pile I made earlier when I cleared the top of the desk, to make a place for people to write if they needed to take notes. I really wanted to get back to the diary and the open Bible. I placed them back on the desktop where I could continue reading. I picked up the diary and began to look at it.

I paged forward and didn't see entries for a while. The next entry was about a month before the fall quarterly meeting.

It began,

> *"Must remember to congratulate Emily Windsor on her very successful Ice Cream Social. The banners worked. We had a number of families who live within walking distance come and share our Ice Cream. Several of the old members said that it had been some time since one of our activities included people from the community. At the Ice Cream Social, Ann Helgeson set up a display to promote Vacation Bible School. Must congratulate Ann for the attendance record she set with the Vacation Bible School. Even most of the parents of the non-member children attended the Friday night presentation that was given by those children who attended the Vacation Bible School. Again, banners seem to be working. Been working with Council to gain support for the tabled items in both Old Business and New Business."*

If I remember right, during this time, Pastor and I were meeting and discussing various things that were bothering him. One thing on his mind was the budget and things to be increased in the budget. He had already talked to Glen Rich about needing a raise in what we were paying him. It is up to the Elders to set what we pay him. The budget for last year didn't have a raise factored in as he had just been called and the Elders didn't think it appropriate to ask the congregation to give him a raise. Now, he was concerned that the Elders were not aware of his financial considerations, and he asked to talk to me.

We met in the afternoon at Denny's. I chose the spot in the corner and asked the waitress to come back when the person I was meeting arrived. When Pastor arrived, he came over to the table and pulled out the chair across from me and nervously sat down.

"Good afternoon, what is it that we need to talk about?" was my greeting.

"My personal budget, a raise for next year," he answered.

The waitress arrived to take our orders. I ordered a Coke and a piece of apple pie. Pastor Chuck ordered coffee and, I think, a sweet roll. She left and I picked up the conversation where we had left off.

"We talked about your budget when you took the call and you thought what we offered was enough to live on," I answered.

"When we talked, I had no idea how my expenses would change living in the greater Atlanta area. I had not factored in the cost of the second car and that the schooling for my kids would be more costly than where I came from. I never expected to get rich as a pastor, but I never took a vow of poverty either," he jokingly stated.

I have found that 'Gallows Humor' is one way to lessen the tension in some stressful situations and Pastor Chuck apparently considered this that kind of situation.

"But that has always been the case. Remember, historically, the monks took a vow of poverty, so we called you into poverty," I laughingly responded.

"It's not that the church hasn't been generous, but things are pretty tight," he seriously stated.

"Well, we did talk about the money during the call, and I remember we kind of promised we would look at it at a later date. Have you discussed this with Glen?" I asked.

"We talked before the last Elders' meeting, but I haven't heard anything back. I believe that the church has moved forward in most areas, but I have yet to be an effective leader in terms of growing the church. With all of the resistance I have been getting, I hope they aren't judging me on that," he responded.

The waitress returned with our order and placed it on the table before us. When she left, I continued, "I'll talk with Glen and see what I can do. We did try to get you settled in when you arrived, we were trying to avoid this problem," I declared.

"The congregation has been very fair," he agreed.

We continued to talk, I don't remember what about anymore, but we finished our afternoon snack and left.

When I got back to my office that afternoon, I did some checking with the District Office. What I found out was that they had been working on guidelines for a salary schedule that churches use to determine what to pay their church workers. They gladly sent me a copy of what they had come up with so far. Their schedule took in a number of factors: a cost-of-living index for the area, number of years active in the ministry, education background i.e., number of degrees and extra training, and years at the congregation. I used their schedule and found that our congregation was significantly under paying our pastor. I took this information to the Elders and Glen made the case for a raise and presented it to Billy Jackson and the Board of Finance.

Pastor and I met one more time before the third quarterly Voters Assembly meeting to discuss the tabled items. The question was how to bring them up at the meeting to get something done. I placed the diary back on the desk.

I leaned back in Pastors comfortable chair and gazed out of the window at the green shrubbery along the lot line between the church property and the neighbors. And the memories came flooding back. Richard Nelson had begun to address the shrubbery around the foundation of the building on three sides so that was no longer a major issue. He had what was there pruned back so it didn't look so wild.

The answer would have been to rip out what was there and start over with new healthy plants, but what he did looked better than before. He did call for volunteers to meet to access the state of the décor in the Sanctuary, Fellowship Hall, bathrooms, and classrooms. It met once and I can't remember the outcome, but no action was taken. Other than that, I did what I could in the Council meetings, but when we met, I think it was to cheer him up.

None of the members were grumbling about anything that I knew of. The attendance at the services was holding steady. The status quo was very comforting for the members, I guess, but the point was we weren't growing. What I remember about that third quarter meeting were all the plans for the fall season. Jo Summers' Youth Ministry Halloween plans, Emily Windsor's big plans for a Thanksgiving event, and Ann Helgeson presented her plans for the children's Christmas Pageant. The adoption of the preliminary budget was contentious with the discussion of Pastor's raise taking up most of the time, but it was passed.

When it came to Old Business though, although some of the items had been addressed through the action of some of the boards. Some of the same tabled items came to the forefront again. The biggest one was the parking lot. Modernizing the church sign was still a committee project. The rest had kind of faded off into obscurity.

The New Business item, the fund drive for the general improvements of the facility was debated and postponed again. That is all I remember of the meeting without digging up the Secretaries Report on that meeting. I reached for the diary and paged to where Pastor had had written his comments about that Voter's Assembly meeting.

I started to read, "*The meeting went pretty well. The congregation seemed pleased with some of the board reports. The budget was…*" My reading was interrupted by the ringing of the phone.

I picked up the receiver and answered.

"Hello, you have reached Shepherd of the Sheep Church, George Harrelson speaking wh…"

"It's me Paul, we just got back to a phone from Jack's cabin," he interrupted.

CONGREGATION PRAYER VIGIL

"Paul, what did you find?" I hurriedly asked.

"They were here and left," Paul replied in a worried voice.

"How do you know?" I asked.

"By what they had left," he answered.

"Are you sure?" I asked.

"Fred is sure. Jack always buys the latest weekly local newspaper when he goes through Dahlonega to see what the County Board of Commissioners are up to. It was lying open on the table in the great room. Plus, there seemed to be fresh Jeep tracks on the driveway and what could have been fresh footprints around where the Jeep had been parked and other areas around the outside of the cabin. We looked for them along the road all the way back to Dahlonega and couldn't see a thing," Paul reported.

"Where are you calling from?" I asked.

"Dahlonega, the pay phone outside of the Lumpkin County Sheriffs' Headquarters," Paul answered.

"Can I speak with Fred?" I asked.

"Fred is busy right now. He is in with the Deputy making out a missing persons' report. We are thinking something happened and they are lost or in trouble somewhere on the mountain," was his reply.

"What are your plans?" I asked.

"That depends on what the Sheriff's Department is going to do. They have already been missing for one night. We need to find them before they are missing for another. Fred wants the sheriff to form a search party. If he does, we will probably stay up here and join the search," Paul explained.

"You are not dressed for that," I pointed out.

"I got over to Fred's about the time he got home from work, and he had just changed into outside work clothes. He suggested that I change into a pair of his Levies as to quote him 'you don't go to the cabin in good clothes'. He also offered me a warmer jacket to wear. I offered to drive, but he said because of the dirt road we would take, it would be better to take his truck. I'm going to go inside and see what Fred is doing. I'll call you back when I know something," Paul said as he hung up the phone.

I looked at the clock, it read 3:17. I had drunk a good amount of Coke, so I decided that before I did anything else, I had to get out of this chair to get some exercise. What better exercise to take than a walk to the bathroom? On the walk back, I happened to pick up a glass of water. I concluded that I felt so tired that maybe this glass of water would keep me awake.

When I got back to Pastor's chair, I picked up the phone and called the parsonage. I entered the number and waited for the phone to ring, but all I got was a busy signal. I waited a couple of moments and tried again. Still a busy signal! I began to wonder what was happening at the parsonage, were they in trouble?

Finally, the phone rang.

"Hello, you have reached the Berg's, Liz Harrelson speaking," stated the voice on the phone.

"Hi, it's me George," I responded

"What have you found out?" Liz hurriedly asked.

"Paul called from the Sheriff's Department in Dahlonega," I began and was interrupted.

"They found them?" Liz excitedly asked.

"No, but they had been there. They are about to leave with the search party the Sheriff's Office is organizing. That's all I know," I stated.

In the background I heard Helen repeat Liz's, they found them statement, with Liz hurriedly answering an emphatic no.

"What's going on? I had to call three times to get through."

"This has been a mad house since I talked to you last! It appears Helga told some of her friends that Pastor is missing. It has now gotten around her group of friends and the phone has not stopped ringing! We have had so many calls from members trying to comfort Helen and asking what they can do that it is driving us crazy! It is comforting for Helen to know she has so much support and the good thing is it is keeping her occupied, but it is still driving me crazy!" she explained.

"We have been trying to keep this thing under our hat until we knew more about what had happened, but I think it is time to activate the Prayer Chain," I said.

"I think we should have done that this morning. It would have saved much of the confusion that has taken place here this afternoon," Liz commented.

"You might be right. Is Clara one of the people who called?" I asked.

"No, I don't think anyone who called was on the Prayer Chain," Liz answered.

"Then, I'll call Clara Bently and get that started," I replied.

I found Pastor's copy of the church directory. With all of the notes he had written by each of the person's name I again felt as though I was trampling on Holy Ground. I felt that this was his private record almost as personal as his diary, so as tempting as it was, I didn't read any notes by any names. I could have gone to the secretary's office and used her congregation phone directory, but I didn't. Seeing as Bently was just a page or two in, I hurriedly copied her phone number, closed the book and placed it where I had found it hoping he wouldn't notice it had ever been opened. I looked at the clock and read 3:45. *I hope she is home,* I thought as I picked up the phone to call her.

As I was about to pick up the phone to call Clara it rang.

"Hello," I answered as I picked up the receiver.

"The Sheriff has gathered a search and rescue team to search along the route that Fred says they usually take. He thinks maybe they had an accident and are trapped some place in the woods. Fred and I are going with them. I'll call you when we find something. We start in a few minutes," Paul breathlessly reported, and the line went click.

I cleared the line and entered Clara's number in the phone. The phone rang about five times before she answered.

"Hello?"

"Hello Clara, George Harrelson here. Have you heard what's going on?" I asked.

"No," responded Clara.

"I have something I think the prayer chain should pray about," I solemnly stated.

"What is it about?" she asked.

"Pastor Chuck is missing. He and Jack Ernst went up to Jack's cabin in the mountains yesterday morning. They didn't come back last night, and no one has heard from them all day. Paul Hessman and Fred Ernst went up to the cabin to see what the problem was. Pastor and Jack had been at the cabin and left. The Lumpkin County Sheriff has a search and rescue team looking for them now. At this point all we can do is pray," I explained.

The line went silent for a time and then Clara spoke, "so he has been missing since Tuesday morning, he and Jack are lost or hurt, and the Lumpkin County Sherriff's Department is searching for them. Is that right?" Clara asked.

"You summed it up very nicely. Can you start on this right away?" I asked.

"I will activate the chain and get back to you with what we are doing," she responded. Where are you so I can call you?" she asked.

"We have set up Pastor's office as the Central Coordination Point, so all the calls concerning this should come here. This is the most comfortable place in the church to work from for the phone to be covered twenty-four seven," I explained.

"Let me talk to my prayer group and get back with you. By the way, is the church open or locked up?" she asked.

"I think I remember locking the door when I got back from McDonalds with lunch," I replied.

"Could we leave the church unlocked if we were to have a prayer vigil?" she asked.

"I think that would be a good idea," I responded.

"Let me talk to my group and get back to you on that," Clara said as she hung up the phone.

I looked at the clock and it was about 4:06 p.m. I tried to call the parsonage to talk with Helen to see about a proper supper, but after the fifth try I gave up. That discussion could wait. I looked at Pastor's couch again and decided if I took just a little nap it might help. I lay down and was out.

I woke to the ringing of the phone on Pastor's desk. It rang for a long time before I could get to it, but I didn't want it to go to the answering machine, so I finally picked it up.

"Hello, Shepherd of the Sheep church, George Harrelson speaking," I stated as cheerily as I could.

"George, it's Clara, the prayer chain has organized a prayer vigil. We will be at the church at 6:00 p.m. and plan to stay until Pastor Chuck and Jack are found. We have formed a phone brigade to get the word out to the congregation," she enthusiastically announced.

"Good, I'll welcome the company," I responded.

"See you soon," she said, and the phone went click.

I tried to call the parsonage again and finally got through.

"Berg residence, Liz Harrelson speaking,"

"It's me George, how are things going?" I asked, I thought I knew the answer, but asked anyway.

"Impossible!" Liz answered in a hushed voice, "the phone hasn't stopped ringing since I last spoke with you and Helen is overcome with worry. The older kids are very worried, and the younger kids are very upset and restless. What is happening and why haven't you called earlier?"

In the background I heard Helen ask Liz who was on the phone and Liz answer back George.

"I kept trying to call but the line has been so busy that this is the first time I was able to get through. Anyway, Clara has organized a prayer vigil here at the church. It will begin at 6:00 p.m. and will go until something happens according to her. What have you done for supper?" I asked.

"Between phone calls we have had time to fix sandwiches, so we have pretty much taken care of supper. What are you going to do?" Liz asked.

"Probably McDonalds again, it was fast for lunch, and I won't starve. I feel I should stay around church for when Paul calls. By the way, would Helen and the kids like to come to church and be a part of the prayer vigil? That might relieve some of the stress to bring them to where the action is. They might not feel so out of the loop, and it will at least give them peace from the phone." I suggested.

"I'll ask," all I could hear were the background noises of the kids chattering and parts of the news on T V.

Finally, Liz was back on the line, "Helen said that she and the kids will be happy to come with me to the church. We will be there probably around 7:00 p.m. She is bringing the extra set of car keys and will drive Pastor's car home tonight," Liz replied.

"That will be good," I responded and hung up the phone.

I had just swiveled the chair to get up when the phone rang.

"Hello, Shepherd of the Sheep Church, George Harrelson speaking. How can I help you?" I answered.

"What is happening?" the voice on the other end of the line asked; I recognized the voice of Glen Rich.

"Here is what we know, Glen. Jack Ernst and Pastor went up to Jack's cabin and basically are missing. The Sheriff has had a search party hunting for them since about 4:00 this afternoon. The Prayer Chain is beginning a vigil here at church starting at 6:00 p.m. That is what we know right now. Paul and Fred Ernst are up there with the search party and will call me here at church when they find them," I hurriedly explained.

"I'll be over as soon as I eat supper," Glen responded, and he hung up the phone.

I had just hung the phone up when it rang again. This time it was Howard Lemke and then Henry Paulson followed by Henry Farmer and Bill Stricker. They all would be coming to pray and help. As the word got around, I got more and more phone calls from members volunteering to help. The way the phone kept ringing I became concerned that if Paul tried to call and update me, he wouldn't be able to get through.

Bill Stricker was the first of the Elders to stop by Pastor's office. I briefed him on what I knew and what was going on here at church. He took over answering the phone in Pastor's office.

"Clara arrived just before 6:00 p.m. and began setting up candles in the sanctuary. She brought a bunch of candles and candleholders to place around the sanctuary. She thought a candlelight vigil would be more appropriate seeing as there was to be no formal service and people would be praying not reading. She was not expecting a lot of people to show up. She had planned that people would drop by and pray for a while and leave."

Liz and Helen arrived soon after Clara. Liz confided in me that Helen couldn't wait to get here so they all just headed for the car after my phone call. I took Liz, Helen, and the kids back to the boardroom and updated them on everything that had happened up until now. Helen had some questions that I couldn't answer, and the kids had some that I could.

One by one, the Elders who knew that Pastor was missing joined us in the boardroom. Glen had called the other Elders so the whole board knew of the problem and eventually all showed up. I asked Liz to cover the phone in Pastor's office and send Bill back to the boardroom. I told Helen and the kids that they could stay for the meeting. I felt that the more they know, the better they would feel. In the absence of Paul, the Head Elder, I held an impromptu meeting.

"Would the meeting come to order?" I asked in a loud voice.

Everyone quieted down.

"Let us pray," I said a short prayer.

"I have briefed all of you on the situation we find ourselves in. Have any of you any suggestions of what we should do now?" I asked.

"I think we should all go home and call the people on our Elders lists and tell them of the situation," suggested Henry Farmer.

"I think that that is the best thing we can do at this time," agreed Henry Paulson.

"Seeing as Paul is up there looking for Pastor, I'll call his list," volunteered Glen.

"Bill, can you cover the phones for another hour? I want to go home and get a shower and a change of clothes. I plan to spend the night again on Pastor's couch. Some of you might want to join the prayer vigil for a while before you leave. Can we end with The Lord's Prayer?" I concluded.

We said The Lord's Prayer, and all went to work on what we were to do.

"Helen, what are you and the kids going to do?" I asked.

"I think we will join the prayer vigil, at least for a while, and then go home. Liz said that if I need her, she will spend the night again. She has been so helpful just handling the phone. The members have been so supportive," Helen answered.

Liz and I went with her and the kids to the prayer vigil in the sanctuary and were surprised by how many people were there. Liz went with me to the office where Bill had already taken over answering the phone.

"Liz, I'm going home to clean up and change clothes. I should be back in an hour, and I will go to McDonalds and get a Big Mac and a coke for my supper. I am going to man the Central Control Point again tonight. Can you man it for a while?" I asked.

"Anything to help," Liz replied.

"Bill, I think you probably should go home and beginning calling your Elders' list," I suggested.

"I agree," Bill replied as he got up from the chair and headed for the door.

Liz went to the Pastor's chair and sat down.

"Good luck with the phones, Liz," I said as I headed for the door.

I got back to the church about 8:30 and heard singing coming from the sanctuary. I looked in and the candles were burning but there was still enough daylight coming through the windows for the people to read from the hymnal. I headed for Pastor's office.

"I'm back. Has it been pretty hectic? Or has it quieted down?" I enquired as I came through Pastor's Office door.

"I think once the Elders started calling and the members got the message, that pretty much stopped the calling. The phone has been quiet for at least fifteen minutes," Liz stated.

"That's good. At least if Paul tries to call, he can get through. Anything else happen since I left?" I asked.

"No, things have settled down in here. There has been a lot of singing taken place in the sanctuary though. I thought prayer vigils were quiet things," Liz replied as she got up from Pastor Chuck's chair.

I placed the McDonald's bag and the Coke on the desk and sat down in the pastor's chair.

"You look refreshed," Liz jokingly said as she ruffled my not yet dry hair.

"Actually, the shower felt good," I responded.

"I'm on my way to the join Helen in the sanctuary and then I'll go with Helen to the parsonage to help out," Liz said as she kissed me on the forehead and turned to leave.

I just got settled in Pastor's chair and opened the McDonald's bag when the phone rang.

"Hello, Shepherd of the Sheep Church," I started to say when I was interrupted by Paul.

"It's getting dark up here and so far, nobody has found anything, so they have called off the search 'til tomorrow morning. They plan to start at about 9:00 a.m. Fred and I are coming home for the night but have promised to come back in the morning. Anything new at your end?" Paul asked.

"The Elders met with me tonight and are calling their lists to apprise them of the situation. Glen is calling your list. Clara and the Prayer Chain are holding a prayer vigil in the sanctuary and from the sound of things, it is going pretty strong," I shared with him.

"Fred wants to get going so I'll talk to you later. Goodbye," Paul said.

"Goodbye," I answered and hung up the phone.

I got out of Pastor's chair and went into the dimly lit sanctuary. I stood there until the last verse of the hymn they were singing was done. Clara noticed me and held up her hand for silence. A hush fell over the members.

"I just got a phone call from Paul. They have found nothing, and the search has been called because of darkness. They will begin tomorrow at 9:00. Paul and Fred are coming home for the night but will go up again tomorrow morning. I am going back to Pastor's office and will spend the night here," I announced.

Clara stood up and suggested that anyone who wanted to go home and sleep should do so as she was going home. She said that she would be here praying in the morning at 7:00 a.m. I went back to the Central coordination Point. Liz, Helen, and the kids stopped by the Pastor's office and said goodbye and left for the parsonage. I took the Big Mac out of the bag and prepared to eat.

ANOTHER NIGHT IN THE DIARY

WHEN I FINISHED MY SPARTAN DINNER, I took a walk around in the building to determine if any of the Prayer Chain was in the building. The odor of the hot wax from blowing out all of the candles they had used lingered in the sanctuary and smelled comforting to me when I went in to check. I found that they had locked all of the doors when they left, and I was alone in the building. After taking care of necessary things, I returned to Pastor's office. I moved the phone as close to the couch as the cord would allow and looked forward to a night's rest.

I felt pretty good considering I had gone twenty-four hours with give or take six hours of sleep. I didn't expect anyone would call, but I wanted to cover just in case, so I moved the phone. I expected a good night's sleep. I lay down on the couch and went out.

I was in a strange town and couldn't find the street where I had parked my car and I was looking frantically for it when out of my dream I heard the phone ring. I reached over and grabbed the receiver, and in my stupor, I answered,

"Hello, George Harrelson."

"We finally got home. Fred and I are going back in the morning. We will be by the church about 6:30 a.m. to pick up Pastor's smelliest robe. They are going to use blood hounds tomorrow and that is the piece of Pastor's clothing that should give the dogs his best scent. Fred has some of Jack's sweaty work clothes to bring along also. You sounded like I woke you up. Go back to sleep I'll see you at 6:30," Paul said, and the line went click.

The adrenaline shock of that phone call had awakened me to the point that there was no way I could go back to sleep. Anyway, I didn't want to have to start looking for my car again! *Hah*!

I got up from the couch and decided Pastor's chair was the most comfortable place to be and sat down. I picked up the diary again and tried to find the page I had left. As I was turning the pages, I happened to turn to a page where Pastor had doodled two small smiley faces and one large frowning face with the tong sticking down out of the mouth. I looked at the date and saw that at this time he was approaching his third year serving Shepherd of the Sheep Church. I forgot all about trying to find where I had left off. My curiosity was piqued, and I had to find out what had inspired him to doodle the faces.

I began to read,

> *"I keep praying things will improve. I'm coming up on the anniversary of my third year and I must look at what has been accomplished. The really big one is the paving of the parking lot which is to be completed in two weeks. I didn't get as many spaces as I wanted, but it is finally being done. It's only taken two and one-half years! I finally got two marked visitor's spaces in the parking lot and the usual people complain that they are unused. The least they could do is invite people to use them! Richard Nelson has done a nice job of sprucing up the property but has not cut down any trees in front of the church. We have some members who believe the trees give the building a homey ambiance and would chain themselves to the trees if Richard came near them with a chainsaw! The church*

sign still looks 'like a church sign should look drab and proper'! We still have not found a community need that we could fill. Is anybody looking anymore? We have tried to open our campus up to community sponsored activities, but that hasn't happened either."

"On the positive side, the Boy Scouts have taken over supervising the walking trails in our wooded area. They made the paths wider and cleared some brush and generally made the trails safer. The confirmation class this Easter again was large. The youth group has been very active and is growing. Some of our youth living close to the church are bringing their friends which is good. Attendance has held steady, at least I seem to be doing something right."

"The number of births and baptisms this has equaled the number of funerals. The number of new members transferred in from other areas have equaled the number of members lost when the paint company in Tucker, GA closed and transferred some members to Baltimore, MD. The church has not grown in the last twelve months. So much for church growth! I have been meeting with George and Howard to try to plan strategies to reach the un-churched people in our community and we have come up with nothing new. The June Voter's Assembly meeting is coming up and my report of the three years I have spent here is going to be 'we are still here', but we have not grown. I guess the dirty little secret for Shepherd of the Sheep Church congregation is to grow we must have more children!"

Oh, what memories those paragraphs bring back. Pastor and I had been meeting just to dream because he had been trying so hard to move the congregation into the mission mode. Then we began to include Howard Lemke in our dreaming sessions. Around the first of the year,

Pastor and I attended a three-day church growth seminar in Charlotte, NC. Howard was slated to go with Pastor, but at the last minute something at work came up and he could not get the days off. I, owning my own business, just told my secretary I'd call in periodically and handle what I could over the phone. That settled it, I went with Pastor.

It was held by a group of Wesleyans and was held at a large church in one of the Charlotte suburbs. It was well attended. I didn't count how many churches were represented, but all of the seats in the church were full. The presentation was good, and it seemed to cover everything that the group, Howard Lemke had taken to Detroit two years earlier, had come back with.

All the way home in the car, Pastor and I talked about ways that we could move the congregation forward to accomplish some of the things that Howard had come back with from Detroit. At least some of the things were still talked about and discussed at the quarterly Voters Assembly meetings. I guess that that trip had lit a fire under me and when I came back, I reported back to the council that we must move forward on the parking lot. That was presented by the Church Council to the March Voters Assembly and over the objections of the financial conservative faction was passed by two votes.

Yes, it was a compromise, Council asked for forty spaces and that got whittled down to thirty. At least that debate was settled, we can now park more cars on asphalt. After the parking lot expansion was approved, there wasn't much objection to the two visitor spaces which were in place the next week.

The subject of thinning the trees in front of the church was opposed by another group of old members and was again put to another committee to debate. The sacred church sign is still there. Banners are costly, but maybe more effective in getting the message out than re-doing the church sign. Also, some of the Evangelical's went crazy with their signs and there is now a county ordinance that covers the square footage limit for church signs.

I remembered how we had tried to encourage community activities to take place on our campus. What we found was that most groups who considered using our facilities found the lack of parking to be the problem. With the addition to the parking lot, we have had more community activity taking place here during the last two years.

Although we don't have a *Boy Scout Pack* active from our church, many of our youth were and still are members of a pack that meets at another church. One of our members was in a pack and needed a project. He took on the project of the walking trail in our wooded area. It still is used by people coming from the neighborhood behind the church.

Compared to the March meeting, the June Voters Assembly that year was absolutely boring. All of the boards gave their reports pointing out all of the things they had accomplished. Pastor gave his report. He pointed out that we were not a growing congregation and that we needed to become more active in the community. He actually had what could have been called a sermon in that report. When it was done, one of the congregation members stood up and made a motion to congratulate Pastor on what a fine job he had done in the three years he had been here. The motion was seconded, and the vote was carried out with a standing ovation.

The Old Business still had the things needed to be done but was ignored and nothing was brought forward to increase church growth in new business. The meeting was adjourned, and the voters went home happy. After reading what pastor had written, I now understand why he left immediately after closing with The Lord's Prayer and not even talking to me. I remember actually feeling good about how the meeting went.

I turned the pages in the diary until I found where Pastor had written his comments about that June meeting.

> *"I survived the June Voters meeting. Yeah. I can't believe it! I have been here, and they haven't heard a thing I have said! We are planted here in this community in this time*

not only to increase in our personal faith, but to spread the
Word. What don't they understand about mission work?
We are called to be a mission in our own community. What
don't they understand about 'go ye there for' anyway? All
I can do is pray!"

It was after that that Pastor Chuck and I began to look at what our Association was doing with its national radio programs aired on Sundays. Pastor decided that he would begin patterning his sermons after the sermons that were broadcast weekly.

I looked at the clock and realized that I had been reliving those days for about an hour and a half. No wonder I felt sleepy. The couch was beckoning to me again. Sleeping in my clothes wasn't a problem, the problem was that it was a little chilly and I could have used a blanket, but instead I curled up tight and somehow that was enough.

It was about 6:30 and still quite dark when I opened my eyes and saw Paul standing in the doorway.

"Wake up, you sleepyhead. We are burning daylight," commanded Paul as I was getting my thoughts together.

"Is it 6:30 already?" answered a voice I hardly recognized as my own.

At that point Fred poked his head in the door and asked, "do you have Pastor's smelliest robe ready for us to pick up?"

"No, I thought you were going to choose," I answered as I got up from the couch and headed toward the closet where his robes were kept.

At that point, I saw Fred's youngest son, Karl, enter the office. As I opened the door, Paul reached in and took the hanger with a white robe and sniffed it.

"I think this one should do," he stated and placed it in the empty garment bag that hung nearby.

"You brought a little extra help along," I said pointing at Karl.

"He was up reading when I got home last night and he asked what was going on. I told him, and he said he would like to come along and search this morning," Fred responded.

"Grampa goes up to the cabin a lot lately and sometimes he takes me along with him. I think he likes company since gra'ma died and we always have a good time. If he is lost, I want to help find him," Karl spoke.

"By the way Paul, shouldn't you be calling around for a fill in pastor? When he is found, after two nights away he may be in no condition to prepare for Sunday's service," I observed.

"I had actually planned to do that today from the pay phone in Dahlonega, but if you wouldn't mind, I'll go out to the car and leave the phone numbers with you," he said and he headed to do that.

"How did the prayer vigil go last night?" queried Fred.

"It was well attended and went on until Paul called to say the search had been called off because of darkness. I think some of the women will be back this morning at around nine," I responded.

"How is Helen taking all of this? I expect that she and the kids are awfully worried?" asked Fred.

"Liz is staying with her and the kids. They were here for the prayer vigil. I think Helen is pretty shook up and Liz is there to help. I think the prayer vigil helped Helen and the kids. The congregation has been very supportive. Yesterday, a lot of people were calling the parsonage and offering help. I don't know if they will be here for the prayer vigil this morning though. I think that will start around nine," I explained.

"That is good to hear. We need all the help we can get. The Sheriff is really baffled as there are no signs that the jeep went off any of the county roads and there are few other places to look. He is going to use hounds this morning and see what they can pick up. There is no way that that jeep could just disappear! Just no way!' Fred exclaimed.

As we were talking, Karl with his hands folded in front of himself was nervously pacing in a small circle in Pastor's office trying to stay out of everyone's way.

"Grampa is a very careful driver. He usually keeps the speed down to 55," Karl injected.

"The CJ 5 isn't a very stable vehicle above 60 anyway and he usually keeps the thing around 45, especially on those mountain roads," Fred stated.

"Here is the book with the supply pastors' names and how to reach them. There are also comments on what they like to preach on and other things about them. I would try Dr. Lentz first as he usually isn't booked up. He is generally pretty busy with his counseling practice and keeps himself available for emergencies. We also should put a bulletin together today. We don't have to put the Hymns in the bulletin as the numbers can be posted Sunday on the Hymn board. We can just list the service page number in the bulletin, so all we need is the other announcements and things that Helga usually puts in there. Was Helga at the prayer vigil last night?" Paul asked.

"I didn't notice," I responded.

"She usually takes care of the bulletin at the beginning of the week and only comes in if Pastor needs something extra done. Today is Thursday, so you better call her and let her know to cut the stencil to and print the bulletin," instructed Paul.

"It's getting late, we got to go if we want to get there before the search begins," announced Paul as he hurriedly went through the door.

"Good luck!" I yelled as they went out the door.

"We'll need it!" Fred yelled back and they were gone.

It was almost seven and my adrenalin was raging. I couldn't imagine getting anymore sleep, so I walked toward the bathroom to prepare for the day. I splashed a little water on my face that made me feel a little better. I should have brought a toothbrush and toothpaste back with me when I went home yesterday, but at that time I still didn't think I'd have to spend the night.

It was almost eight when I got back to the office from my excursion around the church. I was wondering how things were going at the parsonage. So, I moved the phone back onto the desk from where I had placed it near the couch, re-arranged the desktop, and positioned the phone so I could begin my mornings work.

It was now after eight and I really wanted to know how things were going at the parsonage, but the question in my mind was, was it too early to disturb them? Or were they waiting for the latest news? So, I decided to call. I picked up the receiver and entered the number. It rang several times before it was picked up.

"Hello, you have reached the Berg's, Liz Harrelson speaking."

"Hi Liz, how are things going there?" I asked.

"Hi, we slept, but not well. The kids, though, slept pretty well. They are getting ready to go to the special morning program at school, so we have been busy doing what is necessary for them to do that. What is the news from your end?" Liz asked.

"Paul, Fred, and Karl stopped by at around 6:30 a.m. and left to join the search. Other than that, I am alone here at church. Are you planning to come in for the prayer vigil?" I enquired.

"We are planning to be there. Helen and I need to get out of the house and being at church helped so much last night that we decided to come back this morning. If you had called much later, we would have already left," stated Liz.

"Can you stop by McDonald's and pick me up some breakfast on the way?" I asked.

"What would you like?" Liz asked.

"Anything you bring will be appreciated. You decide," I responded.

PASTOR QUESTIONS HIS PURPOSE

AFTER I GOT OFF THE PHONE WITH Liz, I called my office. The phone rang and Rhonda, my secretary and office manager, picked up.

"Hello, Harrelson Insurance, Rhonda speaking, what can I help you with this morning?"

"Good morning, Rhonda. How are things going at the office? I didn't check in with you yesterday afternoon and you didn't call, so I assume things went pretty well," I stated.

"Just the usual renewals and general questions we usually handle, just the normal routine, nothing special," she answered.

"I'm still at church and by the phone if you need me for anything," I told her.

"Are you planning on coming to the office at all today?" she asked.

"I had hoped to come in late this afternoon, but don't count on it. I didn't tell you yesterday what the problem here is. Our pastor is missing and until we find him, I need to be where I can be found. If I don't make it in this afternoon, I will come in Friday to make out the paychecks," I explained.

"Can we here in the office be any help?" Rhonda asked.

"All you can do is pray," I answered.

"Hope you find him," she replied.

"Goodbye," I said and hung up the phone.

I reached for Pastor's church directory again and looked up Helga's number. Again, I carefully placed it back in the spot Pastor keeps it and reached for the phone and placed the call. It rang a few times and until Helga finally picked up.

"Bakemeir residence," she answered.

"Hi Helga, it's George, we still don't know where pastor is, so we need you to come in and put a bulletin together for Sunday. When can you come in to do it?" I asked.

"Probably this afternoon. Pastor usually gives me what the sermon is and the hymns. What do I do about those?" she questioned.

"For the hymns, say see Hymn Board. I don't have a fill in pastor yet so don't put a sermon topic down. As for the service details, just list the service page number in the hymnal and make a note to follow the service in the hymnal," I instructed.

"So, yesterday Paul and Fred didn't find anything?" she asked.

"They found that Pastor and Jack had been at the cabin and then disappeared. Yesterday the Lumpkin County Sheriff led a search party but found nothing. Paul, Fred, and Karl went back to join the nine-o-clock search party. They should start the search pretty soon," I explained.

"How did last night's Prayer Vigil go?" Helga asked.

"We had a lot of people here for it. It went until about nine-o-clock and it's going to resume at nine this morning. Clara just walked in the door, I gotta go, goodbye," I said as I hung up the phone.

"Good morning, George," was her greeting.

"Good morning," I answered back.

"Anything new?" she asked.

"At six-thirty this morning Paul, Fred, and Karl, his son, came by to pick up one of Pastor's robes to give the hound dogs they are going to use today, something to smell. The search should begin at nine," I told her.

"I'm going to get set up for the Prayer Vigil," she said.

"How many people do you expect?" I asked.

"I really have no idea. The number of people that came last night was a surprise. I thought people would say a prayer at home and go on with whatever they were doing, but so many came," she enthusiastically declared.

"I've got to get on the phone and line up a pastor for Sunday," I explained.

"I unlocked all the doors so people should have no trouble getting in," she shared.

"I'll be here if you need me," I suggested as she left the office.

I leaned back in Pastor's chair to relax for a moment. A lot of activities had taken place already this morning and the day was young. I reached for the book that Paul left me with the listing of pastors available to fill in. I was looking at the list when Liz came into the office with my McDonalds bags full of breakfast.

"I brought your breakfast and decided to join you. Helen went to the sanctuary to join in the Prayer Vigil," Liz explained.

"What did you decide to bring?" I asked.

"Two sausage biscuits for you with scalding hot coffee and seeing as I already ate breakfast at the parsonage, a milkshake for me," she said as she laid it all out on the open space on the desk.

"Couldn't you have made it three sausage biscuits for me?" I kiddingly asked.

"You should be happy I'm watching your weight for you," she came back.

I looked at the sparse breakfast laid out on the desk, folded my hands and said, "Let's pray."

Liz folded her hands and together we said the common table prayer. Liz took her milkshake and I unwrapped one of the sausage biscuits. We talked while we ate.

"How were things at the parsonage last night? Did you get any sleep?" I asked.

"We were pretty tired after the Prayer Vigil. I think Helen was emotionally drained and she fell asleep shortly after getting home. I slept in the recliner in the family room. I didn't get much sleep, I just couldn't shut my mind off," was Liz's reply.

"Around six-thirty Paul, Fred, and Karl arrived, and my day has been hectic ever since," I shared.

"Where do you think Pastor and Jack went?" Liz asked.

"I have no idea where they could have gone and not been able to contact someone. After all, Pastor had to be back for his counseling session and he sure would have called someone if he were not able to get back for that. Something had to happen to them. They didn't find them yesterday and all I know is that they should have begun the search for them by now. Did you see any local news? These things sometimes make the news when they search for lost people in the mountains," I replied.

"*Channel 2* news mentioned something about a search going on in Lumpkin County, but we were too busy getting the kids ready for the thing at school. We didn't take the time to listen. It was only a mention, nothing substantive," Liz responded.

We had finished eating and the singing from the sanctuary was getting loud, so Liz left to join the Prayer Vigil. I picked up Paul's book and turned to the fill-in pastors list. I picked up the phone and placed a call to Dr. Lentz's phone.

"Hello, Dr. Lentz speaking. How can I help you?" he answered.

"Hello Dr. Lentz, you may not remember me, but I'm George Harrelson from Shepherd of the Sheep church," I began.

"Oh yes, aren't you Chairman or something, I met you last time I filled in there," he answered.

"Are you preaching anywhere on Sunday?" I asked.

"No, I am free that day, why do you ask?" was his question.

"We may need you to preach on Sunday," I answered.

"Has something happened that Pastor Chuck needs to do on Sunday?" he asked.

"We don't know, but he has been missing since Tuesday and we have to cover for Sunday's service, this is an emergency," I explained.

"I am not preaching anywhere on Sunday but let me check my Day-Timer to be sure I don't have family things to do on Sunday," there was a short silence on the other line as Dr. Lentz checked his schedule. "Looks like I'm clear. Will it be the usual, first service, Sunday school and second service?" he asked.

"Yes," I answered.

"Paul Hessman usually calls me to schedule things. Is Paul alright?" he asked.

"Have you heard about the search for two missing men in Lumpkin County?" I asked.

"It was mentioned in the morning news. No details were given," he answered.

"The people they are searching for are Pastor Chuck and Jack Ernst. They went up to Jack's cabin Tuesday morning and haven't been heard from since. Paul is up there now with the search party," I answered.

"I'll be there," Dr. Lentz replied.

"Thank you. Paul will probably contact you with any details," I said.

"That will be good. I'll keep them in my prayers," he said.

"Thank you. Have a good rest of the day," I said.

"Goodbye," he replied, and I hung up the phone.

I sat back in Pastor's chair and took a moment to relax. The coffee I had for breakfast was finally kicking in and although I was still feeling the effects from lack of sleep, I was feeling a lot better now. I really would have liked to go and join the Prayer Vigil, but if I did that and the phone rang, I wouldn't even hear it. I said a silent prayer and reached for Pastor's diary.

I paged through the diary until I found an entry after the December Voters Assembly meeting.

"This Voters Assembly meeting went really well; all of the boards gave their reports. The election of officers took place and there were there were a number of changes. George Harrelson wanted to step down as President but was re-elected by a standing ovation. Lyndon Caski is now Vice President, Joyce Lyndall is now Corporate Secretary, Harry Hamilton is now Treasurer, and the other big change is Paul Hessman is now Chairman of the Board of Elders."

"The church attendance has been up since the new parking lot was installed. We have had cars parked in the visitor's spaces in the parking lot! We have welcomed new members, but they are people who have moved in from other areas. They are not new members from our community. We haven't been growing from within the community. Our word isn't getting out! We are preaching to ourselves, not to the community! Where have we gone wrong? Is it our message? Is it how we deliver our message? Or is it us and how we come about in our communities? George, Howard, and I are meeting often to try to find ways to reach the un-churched. We attended another church growth seminar held in the Atlanta area and didn't learn anything new! Church growth must be a problem though as so many seminars on it are being offered."

"So far, my sermons seem to fall on deaf ears. The last sermon series paralleled what the national speaker on the association's national Sunday radio broadcast is doing, preaching to the congregation on practicing love and forgiveness. Living as Christians saved by grace working in the community to bring the Gospel to the un-churched seems to be falling on deaf ears. We have become very active, but the activity is inward focused! The outreach isn't happening. Where have I gone wrong? Have I not prayed hard

enough? I feel I was sent here to grow the church and I am
failing! All I can do is pray!"

I read over what he had written, and I remember how the next
meeting after the Voters Assembly meeting with Pastor and Howard
had gone. Howard had thought that that the Voters Assembly meeting
had gone really well. The reports of the progress that each of the boards
were making showed that we, as a congregation, were making progress.
Church attendance was up. Giving was up. He was very pleased that
things were going so smoothly.

I, more or less, echoed what Howard had said.

Pastor just looked at us and pointed out that our evangelism into
the community wasn't working. After that, he took something new to the
Board of Elders. Broaden our outreach with a Saturday evening service.
This was debated in the Elders meetings that followed and even discussed
by members in the church. Half of the elders were for it and half of the
Elders were against it. Pastor Chuck with the help of the Elders was the
one to set the content of the services. Howard stepped in with the recommendation of the Board of Stewardship that we should try adding an
evening service to our services schedule and the debate raged on.

This isn't how we do things! Our fathers would be rolling over in
their graves. The added costs for adding an extra service should be looked
into. Howard and Pastor made the point that in all of the seminars we
had attended, one of the ways for church growth was to find a need and
fill it. Maybe this was the need that this community needed, and the
Saturday service would fill that need. And the debate continued on.

This went to the Church Council where it got a better hearing and
was discussed there. Council took a vote and the members of the Boards
that favored the evening services were Billy Jackson of Evangelism, Emily
Windsor of Social Ministry, Richard Nelson Trustees, Jim Alderson
Youth, and of course Howard Lemke Stewardship. Those opposed
were Raymond Schoff, Financial Secretary, and Lyndon Caski, Vice

President. Those not voting either way were Lois Grenback, Education, and Joyce Lyndall, Secretary. With that vote, the Council supported the pastor.

Pastor, Paul Hessman, and half of the Elders decided that maybe we should try a Saturday evening service pointed at a more youth full part of the community. We could offer that service to the people who had to work on Sundays. This was offered with the 'contemporary service' using what was called the youth liturgy. It still had the components of the liturgical service, but with contemporary music.

The music was supplied by a piano, a guitar, and several people who formed a quartet. Most of the music was modern as not found in our church's hymnal. These services began a week after Easter. Some members of the congregation supported these services and came, but the majority of the members questioned whether this service was really a worship service or just for entertainment.

During this time, Pastor began to preach sermons that concentrated more on what an active Christian should be doing. He was concentrating on doing things to attract people to the activities at our church. He was promoting the Saturday night service as an opportunity to attract more youth and young couples. His hope was that changing the structure of the service but keeping the essence of it could do that.

This did not sit well with the conservative members of the congregation. As I remember this was causing deep rumblings, nothing on the surface. There were people who thought that he was neglecting growing the faith of the members in favor of outsiders. They didn't get the point that they should be growing their faith by witnessing to these outsiders. Pastor was right, they weren't getting the message. This was what led up to the problems.

As I was deep in thought, I was interrupted by Helga walking through the open door.

"Did I interrupt anything? You looked so intent on what you were doing," she asked.

"Oh. Hi Helga, no I was just thinking about what I was reading," was my reply.

"I thought I would come in early to cut the stencil and do the bulletin. I think I'll go and join the Prayer Vigil for a while though before I go to work," she informed me.

"That's probably a good idea. I haven't been in there yet. I've stayed close to the phone. I'm hoping to hear from Paul that they have been found soon. Actually, I need a break and I will join you for a few minutes. I think Clara probably needs all the support she can get," I replied.

We went together to the door to the sanctuary and entered. I was surprised at the turnout. There were thirty-two people there. When we entered, someone was reading from the book of Psalms. Helga went up the aisle and found a seat. I stood at the back and said a short prayer and left.

PASTOR IS ACCUSED OF HERESY

I CAME BACK FROM THE PRAYER VIGIL and sat down in Pastor's comfortable chair. Before Helga came, I had been feeling a little drowsy, but getting out of the chair and walking around had taken care of that. Now, I felt energized and just waiting for the phone call that says they found them.

I said a little prayer and decided to pick up Pastor's diary again. When Helga came, I had laid it down, but the page was lost. I started to page through it again to find that spot, but a doodle caught my attention. It was a stick man hanging from what looked like a string around his neck. That got my attention! Pastor couldn't possibly be thinking about suicide! I put the best construction on it though, and thought it represented a lynching. I just had to read what Pastor had written underneath. It was dated two weeks after the June Voters Assembly meeting.

> "This morning the Circuit Counselor came to visit me at 9:16 a.m. and informed me that charges of Heresy are being filed against me. Heresy of all things! I have been as diligent as humanly possible to follow what the scriptures teach! Lord, my call here is to grow the congregation and that is what I am trying to do. This is an outrage! I have

carefully followed the teachings of our Association on all occasions! I can't believe it! I don't even know what the charges are! These charges are totally unfounded! Lord, I have tried to be faithful to my calling. Have just had a Voters Assembly meeting and I thought it went very well. All of the boards gave glowing reports as to what they have accomplished and what their plans are for the fall. How will the members of the congregation respond to this accusation? Where did this come from? Sure, some of the people in the congregation are not happy with the Saturday night services, but that was only mentioned in the Elders report! Nothing came out about this during the Voters meeting! The circuit counselor said that he just dropped by to give me a heads up that this is happening, and the proper papers are being drawn up. I asked him if we could talk about this, but he said that would have to wait until the formal charges were printed. At that, he decided it would be best for him to leave and he left. Lord, what can they be based on? They must be from in the congregation! Why hasn't the person or people bringing the charges talked to me about this? Going behind my back! I thought they were Christians! Haven't they heard of Matthew 18 verse 15? Am I so frightening that they can't approach me and talk to me? Going over my head or is it stabbing me in my back! I think it is stabbing me in the back! How can they do this to me? Taking it to the circuit counselor! This is personal! This will affect my reputation in the circuit, even in the Association! Who would do this to me? Have I not been giving them my all! Lately with the Saturday night services, sometimes I even spend Saturday night here! Do George and Paul know about these charges? No not stabbed in the back, no, I feel like I have been lynched! Is my pastorate dead? If George and Paul knew about this surely, they would have met with me about this! How can I recover? I will fight this. As soon as I know the charges, I will fight this!"

As I read that entry, it sounded as though he was very upset and was praying as he wrote. I had a vague memory of the day the circuit counselor unexpectedly dropped by to visit Pastor Chuck. I think it was that afternoon when I got the call from him. I don't remember him being excited during the call. He surprised me by asking if I knew anything about heresy. I told him I thought it was something that happened in the Middle Ages. I think I remember him laughing at that.

He then told me that the circuit counselor had dropped by to tell him that heresy charges were being drawn up against him. I think I questioned if he were kidding. Now that I think about that, I am sure what followed was some inane comment. We both had a good laugh; his laugh was probably a nervous laugh, and my laugh was probably based on my thought that this was totally ridiculous.

At that time, I think I passed it off as no big deal. I remember we decided to wait to see what was being charged before we did anything. I had no idea then what he had gone through when he heard that he was being charged. At that time, it didn't make that much of an impression on me that I can't recall any detail about it. What I do remember is when the charges were finally delivered, I think about two weeks later. I turned a few pages in his diary to where I found Pastor's description of them.

"Today the circuit counselor personally delivered the charges of heresy being brought against me. They cover two areas of my ministry. One covers the preaching of impure doctrine and the other covers dereliction of duty. They have been brought by a member who I had great hopes for, a member who could have been very helpful in furthering the ministry of this church in the community. A member

who should have known better! A son of a pastor, Walter Stanke, and a couple of the Elders! I remember how excited I was when Walter transferred his membership to Shepherd of the Sheep Church congregation. I was ready to welcome a fellow worker, one who knew what had to be done, who grew up in a parsonage, and could be a friend and mentor. I had such high hopes! Yet that never happened. He was never ready to take an active position on any board or committee to help in the church. His family attendance was not that regular. They were always 'having to do' something else on Sunday mornings. Yet here he is judging me on the sermons I preach. He, having grown up in a parsonage, should have talked to me about the problems he was having with my sermons! Now, I have to defend my preaching and my doctrinal stance on evangelism and church practice! Some of the charges fall under the designation of adiaphora, church practices neither commanded nor forbidden by God. The circuit counselor has set up three meetings to take place on Sunday afternoons beginning in three weeks at a church in another city. I am to bring copies of six sermons to be 'dissected and judged' by those participating. The people involved will be the District President, the pastors from three congregations, the head Elder from my church and whoever I want to bring and of course Walter Stanke. Six sermons! I don't write sermons; I preach from an outline! How will I be able to be judged on an outline? What can I present? What am I going to do? All I can do is pray."

I remember when the document containing the charges. It was four pages long and had a lot of '*whereas:*' statements in it. I was given a copy and Paul, being a participant, was also given a copy. Paul and I met and read over the document together. We didn't share it with the Elders at that time because we wanted to digest what the charges were and be clear in our own minds what they implied before we shared the document with them.

We were amazed at who had made the charges. Here was a church member, not even a good church member and several Elders who made the charges. Walter, not even an elected Elder, appeared to be their leader. The Elders involved were a part of the old guard and were the ones opposed to the Saturday evening services.

Once we had a good idea of what was written, we had a meeting with Pastor and read through the '*whereas:*' statements with him. Some of them could be classified as nitpicking Pastor for things some of the boards had done and he hadn't stepped in to stop, adiaphora anyone?

In thinking about it now, what it came down to was accusing him of preaching work righteousness. That was preaching about what the congregation could be doing to reach out to the community. And in his sermons, he was echoing what the Association pastor was preaching in his nationwide weekly radio sermons. The other areas addressed were about the Saturday evening services. First it was the hymns, the modern music. Next, it was the order-of-service; it wasn't out of the hymnal. And he didn't wear proper vestments.

Paul and I met with Pastor one weekday morning when Paul took a day off from work and I left my office work to Rhonda. Pastor was trying to assemble his six sermons and make some sense as to how he was going to present them. He said what we were there for was to give him some help choosing his sermons, but I think we were there more for his moral support as we were not experts on any theological issues.

We tried, but he had to decide what he could defend. Our suggestion was to pick sermons for the Sundays he knew Walter was 'having to do' something and wasn't there. We had a good laugh over that, but I chalk that up to gallows humor. I think at that meeting Pastor was relieved that the two of us saw no heresy in anything he showed us. I think in some respect we were the answer to his prayers. He wasn't alone.

The Saturday night and the Sunday after Paul and I met with Pastor at the end of each of the services, I made this announcement.

"Someone in our congregation has filed a complaint against Pastor Chuck. The complaint will be discussed during three sessions being held on three Sundays, at…" I gave the name of the church and its location and then the three dates. "If anyone has any questions about this, contact me or Paul Hessman for answers."

I suppose I wasn't totally truthful about the nature of the complaint, but then how many of the congregation members would even know what heresy was. As it was, a few people asked Paul a few questions and that was it. There was no ground swell of people wanting information.

Paul called a special Elders meeting where Paul and I read over the '*whereas:*' statements with the Elders. Again, there were the Elders attending the meeting who, together with Walter had filed the complaint, but they pretty much remained silent. I had expected some pushback from them, but without their ringleader they really didn't have much to say! Pastor Chuck opened the meeting with prayer and closed the meeting with prayer, but we had counseled him to remain silent and I think that strategy worked.

I paged forward to where Pastor had made an entry after our meeting, the announcement in church and the meeting with the Elders.

"This morning, I met with George and Paul in preparation for my heresy trial. The meeting went well. They were very helpful in choosing the sermons to bring. Walter wasn't specific as to the Sundays he wanted sermons for. George and Paul are very supportive of what I am doing with my sermons, and we have obtained several copies of sermons preached by the pastor on our national radio broadcast. We

have put a pretty good defense together based on what the Association is doing nationally. It really gets down to rightly dividing the law and the Gospel. Do I preach enough law to offset the gospel in my sermons? The first Sunday we meet will be on the sermons. I expect that it will be a long session. In the 'whereas:' statements, Walter wasn't specific to a Sunday sermon, so I don't have a specific situation to defend. I have my outlines which can in each case be read in five or six minutes. Walter will have to pick his objections from the outlines. I feel confident that I am Biblical and confessionally accurate in all of the sermons submitted."

"The next Sunday covers the songs I chose for the Saturday evening services. Those come from a little-known youth hymnal published by our Association and should be acceptable to all who are sitting in judgment. It should be interesting to see Walter's reaction to that information. To make a point, I plan to present the poetic words from several songs without the music to show their scriptural accuracy."

"The final Sunday will be a dissection of the Service I put together. I based it on a service used by the early Christian church. It is a simple formula: Confession of Sins, Praise, Reading the Word, Sermon/Confession of Faith, Prayers, and Blessing with a few of the songs interspersed in between. Granted it isn't from the hymnal, but it is scriptural. After all, the people in our community that we need to reach are the un-churched! This service printed on a handout is less intimidating than having them try to keep finding their proper place in the hymnal. I am feeling more confident that the pastors sitting in judgment will agree with me. As to the wearing of the proper vestments, again, being more informal will be less intimidating. We

want them to listen to the word and not be distracted by
the person presenting the word."

As I read those words, I thought back to those Sundays that the trial took place. I was turning the pages in the diary to find what Pastor wrote at the end of the trial. I found a page with his doodles on top; that had to be the page. If anyone can doodle fireworks, it is Pastor Chuck. The top quarter of the page was filled with little stars and patterns that could only be described as a fireworks display.

Written among the stars and other embellishments in Pastor's script was,

"Thank you, Lord! Thank you, Lord! The vote was
unanimous, I am cleared! I am cleared! Thank you, Lord."

Remembering that late Sunday afternoon in that church in that other town, all I could think of was this fiasco was done and we had a long drive home to church for Paul and Pastor to pick up their cars and go home. Thank God we had won, and he was exonerated, but I was tired and wanted to get home as fast as we could. Pastor was quiet and seemed prayerful, before we left the parking lot, he led us in prayer. I can't remember being as jubilant as what Pastor wrote in his diary. I was just glad it was over, I guess.

For the most part, the congregation was oblivious to the whole affair. It just seemed to go away. Oddly enough, Walter Stanke and his family are still members. The evening services were tried through the summer but never caught on. Some congregation members attended to support it, but no one from the community came and at the end of summer it disbanded.

As I sat deep in thought in Pastor's chair, I was interrupted.

"Hey there, sleepyhead, did I catch you napping?" an ebullient Liz chided.

"I was just deep in thought," was my sleepy reply. Maybe she did catch me napping.

"We came in to say goodbye, we need to get home as the kids will be home from the school program soon and we need to feed them. Thank you for all you are doing. Praying this morning has helped and Liz has made this so much easier," Helen said in an almost tearful voice.

"All I can do is hold down the fort here. I'm sure that they are making progress with the search in Lumpkin County," I said trying to reassure her.

"I know everyone is trying to do their best," she responded.

"I'll call you if I hear anything, just keep hanging in there," was my promise.

"Helen, I think we should leave, I don't want to stretch the speed limit too much on our way home," Liz stated, and they left.

As they were leaving one of the ladies came through the door from the Prayer Vigil and announced.

"We are taking orders to go to Subway for sandwiches. What do you want?" she asked.

"Let me think, I don't do Subways very often. Let's see, maybe a foot long ham and cheese with lettuce and tomato. Yes, I think that would be good," was my reply.

"That sounds good," she answered.

"How has the Prayer Vigil been going?" I enquired.

"There are four of us that are staying into the afternoon, otherwise the people come for an hour or so and leave. In the beginning we had about thirty, but some could only stay a little while. They have been coming in and out and we usually have about ten at any given time," she stated.

"That is pretty good. How is Clara holding up under all the strain?" I asked.

"You know Clara, she is doing fine," she answered.

"By the way, who is paying for the sandwiches?" I asked.

"Clara took up a collection," was her answer.

"Let me add to it," I volunteered as I reached for my wallet and donated a ten-dollar bill.

"Thank you. I think that should help," she said and headed for the door.

I decided that seeing as I was going to be well fed for lunch, I probably should go to the secretary's office and make a pot of coffee. I needed to stretch and walk around anyway. Helga hasn't come by to tell me that the bulletin is done. I should probably go to the church office and see how she is coming with that. While I am there, I can make that fresh pot of coffee if Helga hasn't already done that.

I think coffee will go good with my Subway sandwich. I looked at the clock and it was 11:34, and I was concerned that Paul had not called in with the progress they were making with the search. I extricated myself out of Pastor's comfortable chair and headed for the door. Just as I stepped through the door the phone rang. I hastily turned back and grabbed the receiver.

"Hello, Shepherd of the Sheep Church," I answered.

"We found them!" Paul excitedly announced.

PRAYERS ARE ANSWERED

I was standing in the doorway of Pastor's office when the phone rang. I headed back to the desk and picked up the receiver and as I stood there said, "Hello Shepherd of the Sheep Church." On the other end of the line, Paul's voice excitedly announced, "We found them!"

Receiver in hand, I walked over to Pastor's chair and sat down.

With a feeling of relief, "You did," was all I could think to say.

"They are both alive, there was an accident, Pastor Chuck has a broken leg and Jack is unconscious. We don't know the extent of his injuries yet, but they are in the emergency room at the hospital in Dahlonega and are being checked out. Fred, Karl, and I found them about an hour and forty minutes ago. Karl and I stayed with them while Fred went to contact the sheriff to get two ambulances to us. That took time and now we are at the emergency room. I'll call you back when I know more." Paul said, and he hung up the phone.

I didn't think Helen and Liz had time to get home yet as it was only about quarter to twelve, so I immediately went to the Prayer Vigil group. When I entered, they were sitting in the front pew in silent prayer. I walked up the aisle as nosily as I could to get their attention so as not to startle anyone. By the time I had reached the front, they were aware that I was there. Standing in front of the first step up to the altar, I turned and faced them.

"They have been found and are now safely in the emergency room of the hospital in Dahlonega," I happily announced.

"Praise the Lord! Our prayers have been answered. Let us bow our heads and pray," Clara invited.

The four of us bowed our heads and joined Clare in prayer.

"We thank you, Lord, that they have been found, watch over them and keep them safe until they can be here with us. Amen," was her prayer.

"How were they found?"

"Paul didn't say, except Paul, Fred, and Karl were the ones who found them. Paul is going to call me back and give me more details when he knows something. I think I should get back to Pastor's office and call Helen and Liz to tell them right away. They should have reached the parsonage by now and I don't want to keep them waiting any longer," I told them as I headed down the aisle to leave.

As I left, I heard Clara say to the others, "we might as well wait here for the food we ordered and when it arrives, go to the board room to eat."

As I went out of the door, I think Clara was again leading them in prayers of thanksgiving. I think she probably did that until the food arrived.

I headed to the church office to tell Helga the news and found that she had finished the bulletins and went home. I checked if there was any leftover coffee in the pot, but Helga, in her Teutonic efficiency, had cleaned up and there was the cleaned pot ready for the next time. I settled on taking a glass of water back to the office with me.

When I got back to Pastor's office, I placed my water glass on the desk, sat back down in his comfortable chair, and placed a call to the parsonage. It was almost noon, and the phone rang and rang so when the answering machine picked up, I hung up. I didn't leave a message because if they got home and found a message they would try to call back, probably as I was trying again to call them, and things could get confusing. I waited a few minutes before calling again.

"Hello, you have reached the Berg residence, Liz Harrelson speaking." A woman's voice answered.

"Hi Liz, Pastor and Jack have been found and they are in the emergency room of the Dahlonega Hospital," I excitedly told her.

"Wait! I'll get Helen so you can tell her. Helen, come here. George is on the phone with news," she announced as she handed the receiver to Helen.

"Helen, Paul just called, they have been found and Pastor is in good shape. They are in the emergency room at the hospital in Dahlonega. It was Paul, Fred, and Karl that found them. I don't know any other details yet, but Paul is going to call me here at church when he knows more," I explained.

I didn't know that Pastor was in good shape, but I think Paul would have mentioned it if he weren't and I wanted to reassure Helen that everything would be alright. All I heard on the other end of the line was silence.

Finally, Liz got back on the line, "I think that when Helen heard that good news it relieved so much stress and worry that all she could do was cry. And the kids just came home from the school program so now they are all hugging. I plan to stay here with them until we know more," she informed me.

"Tell Helen I'll call back when I know something. I'll definitely keep the parsonage in the loop," I promised and hung up the phone.

Just as I was wondering what to do next, Lisa, the woman from the Prayer Vigil, came through with a Subway bag in her hand.

"Here is your sandwich," she said as she walked over to my chair and handed it to me.

"Thank you," I replied as I took it from her.

"Here is your change," she said as she tried to hand me some money.

144

"Keep the change and divide it up with the change for the others," I instructed.

"Okay," she replied as she headed for the door.

"Before you leave, you should know that Paul called, and they have found Pastor and Jack. They are in the emergency room at the Dahlonega hospital. I have already told the others and I think they are waiting for you in the sanctuary."

"Our prayers are answered," she happily exclaimed as she hurriedly went through the door.

I cleared a spot on the desktop and un-wrapped my "*feast*". Actually, that Subway sandwich tasted better than I expected and with the water to wash it down, it satisfied my hunger and quenched my thirst. Now, all I had to do was wait for Paul's phone call. The question now was what to do?

I again picked up Pastor's diary and began to look for any entries he had made before the last Voters Assembly meeting. I found a page that I concluded must have been written in preparation for the June meeting. What caught my eye on that page was the doodle of hands placed together in what artists depict as pious prayer, hands positioned palms together vertical in prayer, along the margin of the page.

"Lord, I have prayed for the last months for you to show me a way forward to reach into this neighborhood and minister to the un-churched. The answer to my prayers seemed to be the need for the Saturday night services. I had high hopes for them, and it was an opportunity for the congregation to do some evangelizing in the community, but some in the congregation openly resisted, most of the congregation ignored it and only a few came and supported it. In my sermons, I have been trying to preach outreach. I have been emphasizing going out into the community and yet nothing happens. How can we bring the community

here? I have come upon an idea for a fall festival where we can open-up the back unpaved parking lot and the forested area on a Saturday to the community and hold a small fair. I have discussed this with Emily (Social Ministry), Lois (Education), and Howard (Evangelism). I had a short meeting with George and told him about my idea. I wanted him to place it on the agenda for the June meeting, but he thought it would be better for me to bring it up in my report, therefore I and am going to present it at the June meeting. I also am planning to present a plan for a youth Halloween Party for the neighborhood. I mentioned this to George, and he didn't react one way or the other. I have prayed about these things, but I feel I need the backing of the Voters Assembly before I make the effort to go ahead. I have looked at the statistics and by all standards we are a dying congregation. We are growing only from within and eventually we will become old and wither away! These are the points I will bring up at the meeting."

As I read over what he had written, I thought about the meeting we had after church last Sunday. He had approached me after the service just as Liz and I were leaving. He asked if he could talk to me for a minute. We went into his office and he shared with me what I had just read. I didn't take the time to ask him for details, but I felt that if he took it to Church Council, it would be delayed another month and I agreed that it should go to the voters anyway.

The Halloween thing just kind of went over my head. I should have listened better on that. Really, it has been a long time since Pastor and I have had a dreaming session. Have I been so tied up with my own business that I have not supported Pastor?

He did bring both of these things to the congregation during the meeting. The festival was hotly debated. It wasn't a budgeted item.

Where would he get the money? What is the liability for the congregation to hold such a thing? It is not something that we have done to this scale in the past! The vote was close, but it was voted down.

The Halloween party was remanded to a committee to be looked into. He lost on all of the things he had been praying about. It was then that he told the Voters that unless things change, Shepherd of the Sheep Church is a dying congregation. I thought about what he had written and turned to the page in his diary to read his last entry. This was the page of his open diary that the Bible had been laying on.

He had written,

> "The board reports for the June meeting were very positive and well received. We aren't losing members, thank The Lord. We are inner focused; we are preaching to ourselves. I am praying for a way forward. As it stands now, we are a dying church…"

And that is where he stopped writing. Apparently, he had opened his Bible and that is where I found it.

The Gospel of St. Luke chapter 4 verses 1 and 2.

Verse 1. "*Then Jesus being filled with the Holy Spirit, returned from the Jordan and was led by the spirit into the wilderness,*"

Verse 2. "*being tempted by the devil. And in those days He ate nothing and afterward, when they had ended, he was hungry,*" (Luke 4:1-2, NKJV)

That must have been when Jack Ernst came in and interrupted him. They must have gone to the mountains to pray.

I was pondering that when Clara came in the door.

"I have ended the Prayer Vigil here at church. I will have the ladies call around with the news and ask that people pray for their healing," she announced.

"Thank you," I said.

"Are you going to leave the office now that they are found?" she asked.

"Not until Paul calls back with more information, until then, Pastor's office is still the Central Coordinating Point everyone knows about. I'll probably leave when he checks in. I will call you with the latest news then. I think Paul will have the Elders call their families with the latest news," I explained.

"Well, I think I'll go home and get busy calling my prayer chain. I'll lock up the church before I leave," she said as she left the office.

"Thank you," I called after her as she disappeared down the hall.

Now, all I had to do was wait for Paul's call. It was 11:34 when Paul had called. I looked at the clock and the time was 1:20. The time sure went by fast, but then a lot had happened here at church in the almost two hours since he had called. The pressure was finally off and I could relax.

I awoke in Pastor's chair to the ringing of the phone.

"Hello, Shepherd of the Sheep Church," I sleepily answered.

"Did I catch you sleeping again?" Paul asked in a kind of gotcha voice.

"Yeah, I guess you did, things quieted down here at church, and I guess I just dropped off. What is the news?" I asked.

"Fred and I have been working this pay phone pretty hard. Pastor suffered a shattered tibia plateau in his right knee when the Jeep rolled over. It has taken this long to get the X-rays and to get the leg stabilized. When we found him, he was pretty dehydrated, and in a lot of pain, but other than that he is in pretty good shape. Jack on the other hand was nonresponsive. His clothing was pinned by the steering wheel and couldn't get free. According to Pastor, he was not in a lot of pain, but the lack of his meds caused him to just drift off. He was nonresponsive when the EMT's arrived."

He paused and then continued.

"Fred knew what meds he needed. They treated Jack first and Fred made arrangements to have an ambulance take him to Northside Hospital when he was stable. That's the hospital his doctors work out of. Fred went with him in the ambulance about an hour and a half ago. I have been busy making arrangements for Pastor to go to the Sports Medicine department of Piedmont Hospital where the Orthopedic Doctors work on sports injuries suffered by some of the Atlanta professional sports teams," he explained.

"How on earth did you find them?" I questioned.

"That was why Karl came along. Last night, Karl told his dad that he knew where Grandpa goes when he visits the cabin. It seems since Grandma died, he has been visiting a special place with Karl. It was a special view that Grandpa and Grandma had shared for years. When they got to the cabin, it took Karl a while to find the road leading to that special place, and that is where they found them," Paul explained.

"What are you and Karl doing now?" was my question.

"As soon as the ambulance leaves here for Piedmont Hospital with Pastor, Karl and I are driving Fred's truck to Fred's, and I am picking up my car and driving home. I plan to go to Piedmont and visit Pastor tonight," He explained.

"Should I call the Elders and have them call all of their people to give them the latest news?" I asked.

"No, I've already done that. I told you the payphone here has been busy, didn't I?" he answered.

"Anything else I should know before I hang up?" I asked.

"Have you lined up anyone for Sunday services yet or should I do that?" Paul asked.

"I contacted Rev. Dr. Lentz and he agreed to do Sunday's service. I plan to call him this afternoon and fill him in on what has happened." I responded.

"Good, we can talk with Pastor later to see what he has in mind for the time he takes for recovery. The ambulance is ready to leave so will I see you at the hospital tonight?" Paul asked.

"I will be there, probably with Helen, Liz and the kids," I replied as I hung up the phone.

Now, I had to get busy on the phone. I looked at the clock and it was 3:10. I dialed the parsonage.

The phone rang.

"Hello, you have reached the Berg residence Liz Harrelson speaking."

"Hi Liz, can I speak with Helen?" I asked.

In the background I heard Liz call Helen, "it's George for you."

"Hello," Helen answered.

"Hello Helen, here is the latest. Chuck is in good spirits and is in an ambulance on his way to Piedmont Hospital. He has a shattered tibia plateau. Paul says they have the best doctors to handle this type of injury. The ambulance should get to Piedmont about 5:30 and they should get him into a room by at least 6:30. I assume you and the kids will want to go there and visit him," I said.

"Yes, we will be there!" She responded.

"Can I talk to Liz again?" I asked.

I heard Liz being handed the phone, "Liz, Pastor will be at Piedmont hospital tonight and from what Helen said she and the kids will be there also. What are your plans?"

"Helen and the kids are greatly relieved, and from what I am hearing in the background, they are planning the details of how they are going to do it. Helen has had things pretty much under control since your first call and I don't think she needs me anymore. I think I'll go home and make myself presentable. Are you going to close the office and come home or are you going to stay there?" she quizzed me.

I thought just from the tone of her voice that my answer better be, I'm going home too, and I will see you there before I go to the hospital to see him.

So, I answered, "I have a few things to do here, but I am coming right home, I'll see you there."

"See you soon," she said as she hung up the phone.

I decided to call Clara. I dialed her number and got a busy signal. I waited a moment and tried again, the same busy signal. I decided to wait awhile and call later. Next, I placed a call to Rev. Dr. Lentz. His phone rang several times before he picked it up.

"Hello, Dr. Lentz, how can I help you?"

"Good afternoon, it's George from Shepherd of the Sheep Church and I…"

"Yes, I heard on the noon news that they found the two people that were lost near Dahlonega, alive," he interrupted.

"I just called to give you an update in case you didn't know. Pastor is in pretty good shape for being missing that long but suffered a broken leg and will probably be laid up for a while. Paul and I will be talking with Pastor at Piedmont Hospital tonight and Paul will probably be talking with you as to the future. I just wanted to let you know what is happening," I said.

"Thank you for the update, I'll keep him in my prayers. What about the other man who was with him?" he asked.

"That was Jack Ernst, and he wasn't responding when they found him. His son was with them when they found him and made arrangements to get him to Northside Hospital right away. I don't know his condition," I explained.

"I'll keep him in my prayers also," Dr. Lentz said.

"Do you have any other questions?" I asked.

"If I do, I will give Paul a call," he responded.

"Goodbye and thank you for coming to help on Sunday," I said as I hung up the phone.

I decided to try again to check in with Clara and update her. This time the phone rang and was answered.

"Hello, Clara speaking."

"Clara, it's George. Here is the latest…"

"Pastor is in Piedmont Hospital and Jack is in Northside. My elder called and gave me the latest details. Thank you for calling though. I have so much to do, have a good rest of the day, goodbye," she said as she hung up the phone.

I placed one more call to my business office.

"Hello, Harrelson Insurance, Rhonda speaking, how can I help you this afternoon?" she answered.

"Hi Rhonda,"

"Are you going to come into the office this afternoon?" she asked.

"No, it will be in the morning, I'm just calling to check in," I explained.

"No problems here, everything has been running smooth. Have you found the pastor?" she inquired.

"He's safe and on his way to Piedmont Hospital. I'll tell you all about it in the morning. Have a good rest of the afternoon, or what is left of it, goodbye," I told her.

With that, I hung up the phone, got out of the chair, went through the door to Pastor's office turning the tab to lock it, reached behind me grabbing the knob pulled it shut making sure it was locked, and left the building for home. I hoped these last phone calls hadn't keep Liz waiting for me to get home. It will feel so good to take a shower and get out of these clothes. It has been a long time since I have spent so many hours in the same clothes.

HOW AND WHY

LIZ AND I GOT TO PIEDMONT HOSPITAL at around 7:30. We checked in at the main desk, got his room number, and found that the room was on the third floor. We took the elevator up and approached the room. We checked at the nursing station and found out that Helen and the kids had arrived before he was even in his room and were limiting the number of people who could be in the room with him, so we had to stay in a waiting area on his floor. Helen came out of his room, noticed we were there and came over to talk to us.

"Hi George, hi Liz, I told Chuck I thought you planned to come and visit him tonight. He is still getting over his ordeal in the woods, but he is very anxious to talk to you George," she said.

"We are here for you and him," I responded.

"We appreciate what you, Liz, and the church have done for us. Liz has been such a help and I was so worried. Thank you," she smilingly replied.

"How many people are they letting in the room?" I asked.

"I think the limit is two, but they didn't stop me and the kids, and he was so happy to see us. His spirits are pretty high considering what he went through. He was joking with me about me not seeing the two beautiful sunsets he saw. Other than hunger and pain from his knee,

I don't think he was really affected by the wait to be found. He was talking about being ready to get back to work," Helen explained.

"I am afraid that Liz and I will tire him out, so we don't plan on staying long," I shared.

"He really wants to talk to you. The kids and I should be going home anyway, and it is a long drive. Come with me to the room and we will say good night and leave," Helen invited.

Liz and I followed her to the room. When we came through the door, I was surprised at the room that they placed him in; it was so large. It probably had been a double room at one time but had been converted to a single.

As we entered, to our left were two regular hospital straight-backed chairs. And to our right, toward the head of the bed that was against the wall, was the bed stand where the phone, a pitcher of ice water, and some plastic glasses were positioned. Next to it was the adjustable table that could be moved over the bed. On the other side of the bed was a hospital chair that looked like it could be reclined and made into a bed. On the wall we were facing was a curtained window and below it was the room air conditioning unit blowing cold air. On the wall at the end of the bed were a small table and the doors to the bathroom and small closet.

When we followed Helen in, the kids were sitting quietly in the chairs. The bed was propped up, so Pastor was in a sitting position. He looked at us and the smile came from a face that had had a long day and was a little tired.

"Honey, George and Liz are here. Kids say goodbye to dad. We need to head for home," She instructed as she went to the bed, hugged and kissed Pastor, turned and followed her kids out the door.

"Hi George, hi Liz, pull up a chair and sit down." Pastor Chuck said in a strange sounding voice as he motioned to the two chairs along the wall.

"Hi Pastor," I answered.

"Hi," Liz followed.

We sat down on the chairs.

"Didn't think you'd see me in this good of shape, did you? I think they have me on pain pills and I feel great," he jokingly said.

"Well, we were a little worried about you for a while," was Liz's response.

"Well, I was a little worried myself. Although laying here has given me some time to think so I have a lot of questions for you and George," he responded.

"Probably not as many as I have for you," I answered back.

"Liz, thank you for staying with Helen during the time I was gone. She and I really appreciate what you did."

"It wasn't a problem," Liz responded.

"I am worried about Jack. Have you found out how he is doing? Fred left with the ambulance for Northside Hospital before I could ask about him and Paul didn't know anything. By the way, I told Paul he didn't have to come and visit me tonight, so he won't be meeting you here," he explained.

"I haven't checked with Fred yet to see how Jack is doing," I answered.

"I don't think I will be able to handle Sunday's services. Has Paul asked someone to preach?" Pastor asked as he lay there in his bed.

I now knew why Helen said what she said when we talked as she led us to his room.

"I took care of that. Dr. Lentz will handle the services on Sunday," I answered.

"That's good. He always comes up with good sermons and I think the people like him," he answered.

"Paul and I will talk with you to plan how to cover the services that you won't be able to do when we know more about when you will be able to come back to work," I reassured him.

"Helen said that you kept my appointment with Henry Schoenfeldt and Ellen Morgan. How did that go?" he asked.

"We waited for you but when you didn't come, we talked, and they will make an appointment with you for another time. They seem like a nice couple and will make very good new members," I said.

"Thank you for covering for me. I really don't want to lose them," he replied.

"What can you tell me about your injury?" I asked.

"You are in the insurance business. What is the Association insurance company going to do about my injury? Am I covered?" he asked.

"I haven't even looked at the policy nor have I contacted the District to find out. All we wanted to do was find you, but if my memory serves me right, I think between Jack's insurance and the Association's insurance you should be covered, and if that isn't the case, I think the congregation will help out, too. Don't worry about it," I reassured him.

"That's a relief," he responded.

"What have your doctors told you about your injury?" I again asked.

"The doctors at the Dahlonega hospital showed me the x-rays and said I had shattered the tibia plateau on my right knee. Paul was with me when I was told. He went out to the phone and made contact with the Sports Medicine Department here at Piedmont Hospital. Paul said they are the orthopedic experts in the Atlanta area, and he wanted me there," Pastor explained.

"When will you be meeting with the doctors here at Piedmont?" I asked.

"I don't know. Probably Monday," he replied.

"You guys, all you can do is talk business! What I want to know is what happened?" Liz interrupted with a question.

"The short version is that Jack, in his haste, tried to back the Jeep on the trail and he lost it. We tipped over," Pastor replied.

"Why were you up there anyway?" Liz asked.

"I can see you have spent time with Helen; you are asking the same questions she asked. Jack came by the office Tuesday morning to cheer me up after Monday night's meeting. Helga was there to pick up the bulletin information. We told her that we were going for breakfast at the I-HOP, and I would give her the bulletin information on Wednesday. While we were at I-HOP, I made the comment that what I really needed was a couple hours away from the church to think and pray. It was then that Jack offered to take me up to his cabin in the mountains. He said that there was a special spot that he and his wife visited often. He felt that that place would be a perfect place to do that. It was then that we headed for the mountains. He promised to have me back in time for my meeting,"

"Why didn't you call Helen to tell her what you were going to do anyway?" Liz questioned.

"I should have called Helen from the payphone at the I-HOP, but I didn't think I wouldn't be back in time for the meeting," he replied.

"Well, Helen and the rest of us were pretty worried," Liz scolded.

Pastor Chuck continued, "everything went well, the drive to Dahlonega was pleasant. I had never ridden in an open Jeep before and that was fun. When we got to Dahlonega, we stopped at McDonald's and got lunch which we ate that at the cabin. When we left the cabin, Jack fortunately picked up a cooler full of bottled carbonated water that he wanted to take home. He had an experience with the liter plastic bottles exploding and he wanted to use them before that happened. From the cabin, it was a short drive to this trail which led to his special spot that he wanted to show me. About a mile or so in on the trail we came to a fallen tree that blocked the trail and the Jeep could go no farther. We left the Jeep and walked the rest of the way to a clearing. It was a large rock outcropping that gave a good view of a valley below. Jack and I sat on some logs that he had set up long ago and admired the view. That view was everything Jack had promised. Somehow, the time got away from us and Jack commented that if we hiked real' fast to the Jeep and we got on our way, we could still make it back in time for my meeting. Where the outcropping was, there was enough room to turn the Jeep around. Here on the trail, not so much. Jack started to back the

Jeep back to the start of the trail, but in his haste, he lost it and the Jeep flipped over on top of us. Jack was pinned to the ground by his clothing but was otherwise unhurt. When the Jeep rolled, it bent my right leg and shattered my tibia plateau. Jack tried to get loose but couldn't get to a knife to cut his clothing loose. I couldn't get to the knife either. Neither of us could go to get help."

"Wasn't it painful?" I asked.

"When it happened it was very painful, I think I even heard the bone crack. Once I was on the ground though, as long as I didn't try to move it, the pain was bearable. Fortunately, because the Jeep had no top or doors, I was able to move into a comfortable position on the ground where the pain was much less," he explained.

"But you didn't have food and water? How did you come through so good without it for two days?" Liz questioned.

"The cooler with the bottled water fell very close to where I was laying. I was able to get to it. You can live a long time fasting on water, so we rationed it," he replied.

A nurse suddenly appeared and in an authoritative voice announced, "visiting hours are over, you will have to leave."

"So soon," Pastor complained.

"We have to give you your meds and get you ready for the night," the nurse commanded.

"I'll check on some things and come back tomorrow night." I told him.

"Good night and sleep tight," Liz said as she headed for the door.

"Let us pray," Pastor said as he bowed his head and began to pray.

We bowed our heads and Pastor said a short prayer of thankfulness after which he said, "Good night you two."

"Good night Pastor," I said as I left the room.

Liz and I had a quiet drive home.

The first thing I did when we got home was call Fred. A very tired Fred answered the phone.

"Hello?"

"Hello Fred, how is your dad?" I asked.

"Oh, it's you George, dad's doing better. Once they got the IV in him and stabilized him with fluids and the heart medicine he had missed, he started to get better. I think, though, his doctor wants to keep him in the hospital until they get his blood sugar stabilized, but he is out of the woods. Did you go and see Pastor Chuck?" he asked.

"Liz and I visited him tonight. He is doing well, he's just waiting to see the doctors about his knee," I responded.

"I knew something happened to his knee, but we left before I found out anything," Fred answered.

"He will probably know more details tomorrow. He was worried about Jack though, it might be good if you give him a call and reassure him that Jack is better," I suggested.

"I'll call him tonight. Thank you for calling me, I was wondering about Pastor," he shared.

"Keep me informed on how Jack is doing," I asked.

"Will do, goodbye," he said.

"Goodbye," I answered and hung up the phone.

DECISIONS, DECISIONS, DECISIONS

"Hɪ Pᴀsᴛᴏʀ, ʜᴏᴡ ᴀʀᴇ ʏᴏᴜ ꜰᴇᴇʟɪɴɢ ᴛᴏᴅᴀʏ?" Paul asked.

It's Friday evening and Paul and I have just entered Pastor's room at Piedmont Hospital.

"Hi, Pastor," I said.

"Hi George, hi Paul, I'm feeling pretty good. They keep giving me pills and stuff to keep me happy I think," he replied.

"Well, you are looking chipper," I responded.

"I'm so glad you could both come this evening. We have so much to decide, and I don't want to lay here and worry about these things. Helen and the kids were here all afternoon and I told them I needed to talk to the two of you this evening, so they decided not to come back," Pastor explained.

"What do you have on your mind?" I asked.

"The surgeon came by this afternoon to discuss what to do with my break. Helen was here so we were able to discuss this with him together. This doctor actually was the one that the emergency room doctor in Dahlonega recommended. George, Paul and I looked at the x-rays with the emergency room doctor who thought that this doctor could do the job. In the Emergency Room in Dahlonega, we talked and decided I should take his advice and come here to Piedmont Hospital. Anyway, he has scheduled me for surgery early on Monday to rebuild my knee. According to him, I will be able to move my knee the next day. They have a special machine for that, but I won't be able to put weight on it until he tells me I can. We have to get with the Circuit Counselor and find someone to lead the services until I can stand without help. The doctor said that I will be able to use crutches to get around the house. I will be in a walking cast, but I probably won't be able to walk without crutches for about four to six months. I plan to work out of my office at home as soon as possible. That leaves only the Sunday services where I can't do my job," Pastor explained.

"Rev. Dr. Lentz will probably be able to cover the Sundays until we find someone permanent to cover Sunday services until your able," Paul said.

"I think the Circuit Counselor will be able to help with finding a person to handle what I can't. Paul, contact him and see what he can come up with," Pastor advised.

"I'll check with Rev. Dr. Lentz and see how many Sundays he is willing to cover and then check with the Circuit Counselor to see what we can come up with," Paul responded.

"George, you contact Henry Schoenfeldt and Ellen Morgan; either when they come to church Sunday or by phone and tell them that I will meet with them at the parsonage to continue their membership class and for their marriage counseling so as to not slow down their wedding plans. I don't want anything to discourage these new members," Pastor instructed.

"Which service do they usually attend as I hadn't seen them at church before?" was my question.

"They usually are at early service," he answered.

"I'll look for them there," I answered.

"How is Jack doing? Fred called last night to give me an update and he was doing pretty well then, but have you heard anything more?" Pastor asked.

"I called Fred before I came tonight and he is doing well enough to be discharged tomorrow afternoon," Paul said.

"He had me worried before we were found. I spent a lot of time praying for him. I'm glad he is doing okay," Pastor replied.

"Two days without food and water can take a toll on anyone, but on an eighty-two-year-old man it could have been bad," I observed.

"For me it really wasn't that bad. We had had a good McDonalds' meal for lunch on Tuesday at the cabin. Then we headed for that special spot. After the accident, we had the cooler which was filled with liter bottles of seltzer water. So, all we lacked was food. After the Jeep rolled over, the cooler landed within the reach of my right arm so I could get the bottles out and pass them to Jack. After everything settled down and the initial pain in my knee subsided, I couldn't move without causing more pain. Jack wasn't in any pain but the edge of the body of the Jeep had pinned some of his clothes to the ground and it was as though he was tied in place. With no top on that Jeep, when it rolled, we were in danger of being crushed by the sides of the body. Fortunately, the windshield and some trees kept the body from going totally to the ground on my side, but that was what pinned Jack's pants," Pastor explained.

"You had to see it to believe it, the way that body was situated on the ground. Had it not been for the trees and the fact that it had no doors it could have crushed them both. Jack was half in and half out from under the Jeep's body through the door opening. The way the windshield supported that side of the Jeep gave him extra room to move about. Fortunately, that Jeep is a 1956 CJ5 and doesn't have the high seat backs. That gave them more room to maneuver around under there. The passenger side was leaning against the side of a good-sized tree and came to rest about three feet above the ground. Pastor was more or less lying under the body outside on the passenger's side. Had the Jeep body not been wedged against the tree trunk, it would have probably crushed him. He was fortunate to have landed on leaves and ferns and not on the jagged rocks nearby. As it was, it really formed kind of a bed for Pastor and a shelter for both of them," Paul added.

Pastor began again, "after we rolled, we took stock of the situation. The Jeep was basically upside down so first we checked to find any leaks. The fear was if gasoline was leaking it could burst into flames at any time. The gas cap held, and we didn't smell gas. Next, Jack tried to wiggle out the clothes that were caught in the door opening pinning him to the ground. The way the Jeep landed it had pushed the leg away so it would not be crushed, but the baggy pants leg was caught under the edge and pinched the leg. He was able to loosen the pinch, but the pants still held tight. There was no way to wiggle his leg out of the pants. Try as he could, the denim his pants were made of would not rip. He figured that all he had to do was get loose and he could go and get help. There was nothing sharp we could get to that he could use to cut the material, so we decided we would have to wait to be found. Jack said not to worry, he and his grandson Karl went to that special place often and he was certain that when they started to look for us Karl would know where to find us."

Paul interjected, "Jack was right about that. Karl was sure that he knew just where you had gone. He said that every time he went to the cabin with Grandpa they would go there and remember Grandma."

Pastor continued, "It was lucky that Jack had packed those bottles as the cooler landed near where I was on the ground. It was painful, but I was able to wiggle over to it and get the bottles out. Jack figured that they would find us on Wednesday, but we should ration the water to have some left for Thursday in case it took that long. We did pretty well with the water, but it was the lack of food the concerned Jack. He is diabetic and he was not concerned that his blood sugar would go low because all he had to do to prevent that was not take his pills. His concern was how high it would go. Also, he didn't have his heart meds and he didn't know how long he could last without them. Other than the mild throbbing pain from my knee, I found a comfortable position to lie in as long as I didn't move around very much. I was able to get a bottle of water to Jack, but we decided not to drink much as that would lead to peeing and from our positions that was messy for both of us."

"That evening we talked about things at church, sang several hymns, and prayed. We fell asleep to the sounds of the crickets and other insects. It was a warm June night and although I woke several times to noises around me, I slept pretty well. We awoke to the normal forest noises. Because of my waking up in the middle of the night, I asked Jack about bears and other mountain animals that might harm us. He laughed and told me not to worry, that they were probably more scared of us."

"We spent most of the day praying, playing word games, wondering how soon the searchers would find us. Just to be helpful though, we took turns each hour calling out for any searchers to find us. The hunger was getting to me. Jack told me to drink a little water when it got bad and that seemed to help. As long as I didn't move, my knee didn't hurt, it only throbbed which was something I was getting used to. We just kept waiting."

"Jack became pretty sleepy, bordering on unresponsive around sunset and I became rather worried about him. I tried to keep him talking. I encouraged him to drink more water, but from my position I couldn't tell if he had done so. I prayed myself to sleep that night."

"When I awoke in the morning, I tried to arouse Jack, but he was unresponsive. From my position, I could see his clothes moving so I knew he was still breathing. I woke up to hunger and the water I drank didn't seem to help. My knee was still throbbing, but either it was getting better or I was getting used to that feeling. I think the hunger bothered me more than the knee. I pretty much spent the morning knapping and praying. I think it was a little afternoon when I heard Fred calling as he was running toward where we were. I was ecstatic to hear the voice and in my loudest voice called back. He was joined by Paul and Karl."

Paul turned to me and adding, "Karl found the trail and Fred tried to drive the truck on it, but right away the trail was too narrow for the truck, so he parked it and we began to walk into the woods. As soon as we got a little of the way in, he told us that he thought he saw the Jeep and began running on the trail ahead of us. Karl and I began running behind him."

Pastor picked up the thread.

"Fred checked Jack and then left to get the ambulances. Paul and Karl tried to free up Jack's pant leg but were concerned that moving anything would cause the Jeep to move and crush Jack. We had to wait for about an hour for the ambulances to get there and walk the litters back to the wreck. It was so good to talk to someone that that hour went by really fast. When the EMT's arrived, they placed me on a litter and took me the painful distance to the ambulance where they stabilized my leg for the ride to the Emergency Room. The hospital is on the top of a mountain and on the road leading up to it is the place where the McDonalds where we stopped to get our dinner on Tuesday is located. I begged for them to stop, but to no avail."

Paul chimed in, "when pastor was clear it took five men to lift the Jeep so that Jack could be pulled out. Fred went with the litter and the ambulance to the Emergency Room. Karl and I brought Fred's truck back."

"I wondered how they got Jack out from under. Now that I have had time to think about it, it was a miracle that neither of us was killed," Pastor observed.

"I thought the same thing when I saw the wreck," Paul stated.

"George, did you check on the status of our church insurance yet?" Pastor asked.

"I put in a call to the District but haven't heard back yet. I haven't even brought it up with Fred. I thought I would check with Jack seeing as he is better," I responded.

"George, Helen told me about your spending the two days in the office coordinating the search. She also told me about Clara and the Prayer Vigil. I have a statement that I would like you to read to the congregation Sunday after each service," Pastor said as he handed me a piece of paper. "Helen and I have appreciated what all the congregation have done for us this past week. Thank you," an emotional Pastor Chuck said.

"Visiting time is over, it's time for his meds," a nurse announced.

"Let us pray," Pastor said as he folded his hands and began, "Heavenly Father we …"

THE FUTURE

"Hi Pastor Chuck, how are you feeling this afternoon?" was my question as I entered his hospital room.

It is Saturday afternoon and Pastor invited me to come and visit with him. I felt that Helen and the kids should be the ones here, but when I talked to Helen about it, she told me that Pastor had had so much time to think that he is really needing to talk with me.

He looked at me from the bed which was positioned to have him propped up in a half sitting position and answered, "Hi George, the drugs are taking care of any pain I think I should be feeling. I am glad that you could come this afternoon. Pull a chair closer to the bed so we can talk," he suggested.

"I am here to help any way I can," I responded as I pulled one of the straight-backed chairs closer to the bed.

"It's just that I have been thinking about a lot of things, about the church, about my accident and about my future. These are the things that are going through my mind as I lay here. We just need to talk," he explained.

"Relax, don't worry about the insurances, I think that all of this will be covered," I said as I tried to reassure him.

"Helen told me that you found my Bible lying open on my diary on the desk. When I was missing, she told me that she encouraged you to look through it to see if it would shed some light on where I was. How much did you read?" he pensively asked.

How could I answer? I felt the sense of guilt come back to me as when I first was tempted and then began reading. Now, Helen had told him that I had looked in the diary. I knew when I did it, I felt it was wrong, but out of curiosity I did it anyway. I felt embarrassed and I am sure the color went out of my face as he asked. I am sure, not knowing how much I had read, that he felt compromised. What could I say? I had to answer truthfully.

"I looked through it and read some of the entries," I sheepishly confessed.

"Did you share anything you read with anyone?" he asked.

"No," I answered.

"I understand your desire to find out what happened to me, but I also feel you violated my trust in you and I feel compromised! Those thoughts were between me and God. If Helen hadn't told me that you had looked in my diary, would you have told me?" he questioned.

What could I say to repair the damage I had done?

"Yes, I would have told you as you would have noticed that the book had been used. We were all very concerned and were looking for any indication that you were not abducted or somehow in trouble. We were all so very concerned. I am sorry that I violated your privacy and I ask your forgiveness. I didn't read anything there those compromises anything in your ministry," I emphatically added.

"Then I forgive you for invading my privacy," he pronounced.

"You have my total support and whatever I saw will remain sealed," I reassured.

"Pray with me," Pastor commanded as he folded his hands and began to pray.

"Amen," I said at the end of the prayer.

Pastor got a serious look on his face and said, "Monday night's meeting was a disaster. I have prayed and prayed to the Lord to lead me to something to get us deeper into the community. I have worked with Emily and the Board of Social Ministry to come up with ideas to go out into the community and she brought in Evangelism and Howard was very enthused. Howard talked to Lois, and she brought it to the Board of Education, and they thought it thought it was a good idea. Think of it, we have the land with the woods. We have opened it up and it is like a community park! We already have the trail through our woods that is used by people from the next street over to get from street to street,"

"And a lot of people are using it. I think it is well known in the community," I agreed.

"Think of it, a Fall Festival, a place on our campus that could welcome the whole community! A part of our community that don't already frequently use the trail. I didn't bring you into the plan because I wanted the boards to be responsible and initiate the project. The boards didn't bring the plan to council because it wasn't complete or ready yet for the negativity it would have had to face there. When I asked you about it you thought it would be better accepted if it was part of my report. I agreed with you. Here we put together a plan with support from three boards with the hope that the voters would back it and we would have enough time to put together a first-class festival and what happened? The old guard shot it down," he stated in a voice that dripped of defeat.

"Well, there was a debate," I injected.

He continued, "I took a lot of time planning my report. I laid out the statistics on the growth pattern that Shepherd of the Sheep Church has had for the five years I have been here, and it doesn't look promising. We are inner focused! We are serving ourselves and not the community. The new members we get generally come from transfers to the Atlanta area. Granted we have the children of the members, but once they leave home they move away for college, jobs, and opportunity.

By all the church growth statistics, we are a dying congregation. With censes numbers for our community telling us that half of the members of our community are un-churched, all we should have to do is reach them with the gospel. Here, with the festival, we could have had the opportunity to welcome the community and expose them what we have to offer. What is the liability? That is a new one! Where will we get the money, they ask? When asked, somehow the Lord provides. Yes, it was a debate! The old guard came through strong. We didn't lose by much, but we lost! We still have a chance for the Halloween thing. We as a church have lost our vision. Where is go ye therefore?" Pastor looked flush when he finished talking and then he sighed.

I sat there with him in silence for a while. Everything he said was true. I think he had to get it off his chest. I, a salesman, was caught without words. We looked at each other in silence for a while. Pastor was pouring out his heart to me and I couldn't find words to comfort him with.

Then he continued, "I remember my call to Shepherd of the Sheep Church. It was twofold. The first part was to grow the congregation in personal faith. The second part was to be the Evangelistic leader to bring The Word of God into the community. From everything I saw during Monday night's meeting, the congregation is perfectly happy with what the boards are accomplishing. They seem to be perfectly happy with what I have done. They seem to be perfectly happy to keep their faith bottled up in this closed church community and, it seems, some even seem fearful of outsiders coming in and disrupting their community of faith! So, from their standpoint I am doing exactly what I was called to do! But didn't they write my call? My call was to also bring the Word into the community. Yet every time I have tried, I have run into a stone wall. That was what frustrated me Monday night. My prayer is: what is it God wants me to do here? Is my ministry here done? Do I need to bring up my call to the congregation and ask for a reaffirmation of that call? Should I consider putting my name on a call list? These were things that I have been praying over. These were the questions I needed God to send me answers for."

"After the meeting, Jack Ernst came up to me and gave me a pat on the back and asked me if I wanted to talk. For my whole time here, I have known the Ernst family as stalwarts of the congregation, but they were never on any boards, and I never found a reason to be close with them. They were just there. When Jack came to me after the meeting, it was a surprise. I didn't know what to think. He said that he would drop by my office in the morning, and we could get breakfast together. I was tired and the trip home and driving back in the morning would take time, so I decided to sleep on the couch in the office. I called Helen and told her that I was tired and would sleep there."

"You didn't tell her you were meeting Jack in the morning?" I asked.

"I was tired, frustrated, maybe even mad and I thought that after breakfast with Jack I would go home around noon. No, she had no idea," Pastor confessed.

"Well, she was very worried," I shared.

"Oh, I have been properly 'chewed out' about that," he replied.

"We didn't know about Jack's visit until Wednesday when we found out about it from Helga," was my response.

"Monday night I prayed for a while before falling asleep. I questioned my call. I questioned the congregation's commitment. I asked for guidance and help. No answers came out of the blue. I woke early and was still upset so I started to write in my diary. I picked up my Bible and it opened to where a book marker had been placed some time ago. It opened to the Gospel of St. Luke, Chapter 4. The first words my eyes focused in on were Chapter 4, verses 1 and 2. And I began to read. I read it again. I picked up my red pen and underlined verses 1 and 2. I think I thought a silent prayer wishing that I could go up to the mountains and pray. As I was looking at the Bible as it lay open on top of my diary, Jack knocked at the office door, and I invited him in. It was about 7:30 when he came. During the meeting, he had been one of the people that thought the Fall Festival was a good idea and could be the beginning of a tradition. Really, I think he came to comfort me and share with me a little history of Shepherd of the Sheep Church. Were you here at the founding?" Pastor asked.

"No, Shepherd of the Sheep Church was the church that our pastor in Minnesota recommended we find when we moved to the Atlanta area. I came from a small town outside of St. Paul, Minnesota, Woodbury. A Minnesota insurance company wanted to get a foothold in the south and convinced me to come here and start it. When we arrived, Shepherd of the Sheep Church was well established," I explained.

"Well, Jack explained that this bunch of Germans, Norwegians, Swedes, and other Northern Europeans in the area got together and formed a church based on their common confessional heritage. Their whole emphasis was on maintaining 'doctrinal purity' presented in 'good order'. Jack's father was one of the founders. Jack explained there are actually three factions working in the church and there might even be a fourth one. There are the doctrinal purists, the financial protectionists, and the evangelists. The new faction would be the young new members, the ones that scare the other three, the pragmatists, who just want to get something done. Two of the factions are hanging on to the past. In that respect, the very desk in my office at church is a 'holy relic' as it came from Jack's father's office at the hardware store," Pastor jokingly explained.

"It is a very ornate beautiful piece of furniture, and I knew that it had come from the Ernst family, but I never knew it was a 'holy relic'," I laughingly responded.

Pastor continued, "going back to the history of the church, it grew not from the community but from people like yourself transferring from someplace else. Henry Schoenfelt is the prime example, and he is growing the church by marriage! Hopefully, in the future they will grow this church by having several children. Most of the 'new members' have come from people transferred into this area by GM, Ford, and the other large corporations that have large operations here. The Ernst family is unusual in that most of the family has found employment here and remained in the area. Most of the youth from our church have gone away to college and when graduated, have found work far from where they were raised. If this trend continues, we are indeed a dying church. Jack and I spent a lot of time discussing those problems."

"We have discussed those problems also," was my defensive comeback.

"But not in those terms, we have discussed church growth and you have worked with me to try to make that happen, but we have never discussed the root causes of the problem in the first place. Anyway, Jack and I continued to discuss those problems during breakfast at the I-HOP. That was when I mentioned to Jack that I really needed to go someplace away from here where I could pray. Jack told me that he knew just the right place to do that, the very special place where he and his wife used to go to pray. We talked about it, and I thought of the very Bible verse I had read when he knocked on my door. I had no idea that I would be given the opportunity to fast and pray for two days. I accepted his invitation with the condition that we be back for my 8:00 o'clock appointment with Henry Schoenfelt and Ellen Morgan. The ride up to the cabin in an open Jeep was very refreshing. If I ever get the courage to ask Helen, I will try to find a Jeep, but I am afraid that that idea will go the way of the motorcycle I once wanted," he dreamily explained.

"I flirted with the motorcycle idea once but being in insurance and seeing the statistics, I gave up the idea. As far as I know the Jeeps are pretty safe though." I commented.

"After we were stopped by the log in the path, and it was so narrow that only a jeep could go through, Jack and I walked to the spot. Jack and I prayed together and then Jack left me alone for a while to meditate. I wasn't watching the time and we were running late, but you know that. After the accident and we found out we would have to wait to be found, during that time, Jack and I, for the first time, became very close." Pastor shared.

"The Ernst family as one of the founding families of the church and have been faithful members as long as Liz and I have been here. My impression was they wanted to support the church and be there but wanted to make room for the newer members to be active in leadership roles, so they stepped aside. They are some of our strongest givers," I explained.

Pastor's face became very serious, and he looked straight into my eyes as he continued, "George, talking to you, sharing with you, and depending on you has been a good working relationship. I look at you as my brother in the ministry. Jack came to me as a fellow Christian and over the past few days became like a father to me. I believe God moved him to come to me when I was at my lowest moment in my ministry. He was there when I needed him."

"He gave me insight that comes with the history of the congregation that I have been serving for the last five years. I shared with him my questioning of my call and asked him why he hadn't come to me sooner with the history that he had just shared. He explained that it was the future that he expected me to bring to the congregation not the past. He had long ago concluded that we were a dying congregation and we needed new leadership from the outside to reverse that. He didn't want to taint me with the old or to influence me in any way, he wanted new ideas."

"His thoughts are that the young people in the church are not too busy to pitch in, but he feels that the older and mature members have frozen them out. We, old people, are not training our replacements. He asked me if I noticed that with each of the elections for officers each cycle, that the older members didn't recruit new people to run for the offices, they ran the people that held the position and only asked for nominations from the floor. An Example is Emily Windsor. She has held that job since it was created."

"The only way there is new blood is for one in a leadership position to retire. The last election when you were re-elected as President is a good example. There was some shuffling of the boards, but none of the younger members were asked. Harold Lee didn't want to replace you then; he just wanted to go back and sit in the pew. Lyndon Caski stepped up to be Vice President, but he was active as a member of another board. I hope you are training him to lead." He looked at me earnestly.

"You make a good point, I did look around, but no one put their finger in the air, and I ran again," I responded.

"Jack and I explored the congregation's commitment. The attendance is up. The giving is up. There are no issues that are coming from the congregation. But we are not growing from the community. This is what I have been praying about. That was the reason I began working with the boards to move the congregation to do more outreach. So, I reasoned what board is better than Social Ministry to look the needs of the community. Find a need and fill it, isn't that the way out into the community?"

"That is what all of the church growth consultants have been saying and we heard that from the people who went to Michigan," I responded.

"So, I looked to the Board of Social Ministry. Then I asked myself isn't it the Board of Evangelism that focuses on spreading the Word into the community? What can they do to better accomplish that? Then I looked to the Board of Education for the Sunday school as a way of approaching the community again, but through education. All of these things could have been showcased at our Fall Festival with small booths," he explained.

"I agree," I said as I nodded my head.

"On Wednesday, Jack and I had talked about expanding our youth program and possibly calling a professional youth minister. Jim Alderson has been doing a great job with the Board of Youth Ministries, but if we could expand our youth activities this might be an avenue into the community. I think he was trying to look to the future and get me thinking positive thoughts. Then Jack got serious and asked me with the way things were going, if I was planning to put my name on a call list. At that time, I told him that I was considering the idea and that was one of the things I was praying about. We prayed together about that. It was after that when he started to drift off. Thursday morning, Jack was silent. I drank some water to help with the hunger and spent time in prayer until I heard Fred come," he bowed his head, sighed and was silent.

I sat there with him again not knowing how to respond. He was sitting propped up in the bed with his head bowed taking slow and measured breaths. I was wondering if his drugs had worn off and he was in physical pain. Then as I looked at him, I realized that indeed he was in pain, but it was the pain caused by *failure*, by *indecision*, and by '*the looking for answers that weren't easy to find*'.

"What can I do to help?" I asked.

Pastor raised his head and looking at me with a determined look stated, "The reason I wanted to talk with you today is that through my prayers I have come to realize that we, you and I as leaders in this church have to 'lead'. During my recuperation, I will have the time to put a plan together a plan as Jack suggested; for a youth minister to help Jim Alderson grow the young people in this congregation, not only the youth, but the young families. His job will work with me to grow the next generation of leaders in Shepherd of the Sheep Church congregation. I will need your help to do this. I will need the Church Council to be behind this. Will you pray with me about this?" he pleadingly asked as he bowed his head and folded his hands.

I bowed my head and joined him in prayer.

When the prayer was ended, I said, "Pastor, I will work with you and support any plan you will make."

"Thank you. I feel tired and I think I need a nap," a tired face looked at me and turned to face the wall.

"Have a good rest," I said as I got up from the chair and headed for the door.

EPILOGUE

PASTOR CHUCK'S SURGERY WENT WELL. THE DOCTOR put the shattered tibia plateau together with a plate and seven screws. His leg was placed in a removable cast which allowed him to be able to bend his knee joint for exercise and with the cast in place, get around the parsonage with crutches. George kidded him by referring to him as his '*bionic preacher*'.

Within a few weeks, Pastor Chuck was working full time from his '*home office*' in the parsonage. After a few months, he was walking around using one crutch, and in six months, his doctor gave him a prescription to come back to work! Little did the doctor know that Pastor Chuck had been working from home as soon as he could sit comfortably in a chair.

George and Paul worked with the Circuit Counselor and were able to find a retired pastor who could lead the Sunday services and signed him up to a six-month contract. At the beginning, he led the services and preached but as soon as Pastor Chuck could stand for thirty minutes without his crutch, the retired pastor still led the service but Pastor Chuck would deliver the sermon.

Pastor Chuck continued his new member meetings with Henry Schoenfeldt and Ellen Morgan. One of his first acts when he came back to fulltime status was to officiate at their Christmas wedding. Jack

Ernst was out of the hospital and *'up and at it'* the next week. He and Pastor became very close, and he was a frequent visitor at the parsonage during Pastor Chuck's recovery. His Jeep has recovered and surprisingly was easily repaired. However, it took quite a bit of time and energy to *'square things'* with The Department of Natural Resources over driving his Jeep on mountain walking trails.

Fred had Pastor's *'smelliest robe'*, the one they had taken to Dahlonega for the dogs to smell during the search, sent to the cleaners and he and George placed it in its proper closet in the office. George also, after having discussed it with Pastor Chuck, rearranged the top of Pastor's desk so as to make it useable to the Pastor who was leading the services.

As soon as Pastor was *'up to it'*, he and George began working on the plan to present to the congregation the request for the creation of a Youth Minister position. During this time, they were able to research the successful programs in other churches. As they moved forward with their plans, they included Jim Alderson, Chairman of the Board of Youth Ministries; Lois Grenbach, Chair of the Board of Education; Howard Lemke, Chairman of the Board of Evangelism; and Paul Hessman, Chairman of the Board of Elders.

With the congregation experiencing the effect of having their pastor and someone to assist him, they had become very comfortable with the idea of another fulltime church worker. George was of the opinion that this positive experience would be helpful in convincing the church to create the full-time position of Youth Minister. And with the spring Voter's Assembly Meeting on the horizon, George and Pastor Chuck decided that the plan was ready to present to Church Council for approval to be placed on the meeting agenda.

Now, was the time to lead!

www.ingramcontent.com/pod-product-compliance
Lightning Source LLC
Chambersburg PA
CBHW071356120626
46546CB00002B/723